FACING PROTESTANT —
ROMAN CATHOLIC TENSIONS

FACING

Protestant—
Roman Catholic

TENSIONS

How to think clearly about them as suggested
by leading Roman Catholics
and Protestants

EDITED BY WAYNE H. COWAN

ASSOCIATION PRESS • NEW YORK

CONTENTS

5

ACKNOWLEDGMENTS

The editor wishes to thank the following publishers for permission to reprint from their publications:

Charles Scribner's Sons for permission to reprint John C. Bennett's "A Protestant Looks at American Roman Catholicism," which appeared as part of a chapter in his book *Christians and the State*; The Macmillan Company for a passage from *Catholic Principles of Politics* by John A. Ryan and Francis J. Boland; Beacon Press for a passage from *American Freedom and Catholic Power* by Paul Blanshard, and also for a passage from *Protestant and Catholic* by Kenneth Underwood.

FOREWORD

Facing Protestant — Roman Catholic* tensions is, judging by a glance at the daily newspaper, something on which Americans spend a great deal of time and energy. It is important, therefore, that this be done in the most constructive way possible for the benefit of all. Otherwise, as we have too often learned, the total society suffers.

Let it be stated at the outset that tension is a natural product of life in a pluralistic society. Where groups of different religious backgrounds and traditions live together, a certain amount of tension in the civil society is both inevitable and healthy. It would be foolish to expect the situation to be otherwise. Whether it should take the forms it does, whether it need rend the fabric of our society as it frequently does, however, is certainly a question that deserves considerable attention.

The purpose of this book is to help the concerned reader to identify and understand these tensions and what underlies them, to help him sort out those that

---

* For convenience, the word "Catholic" rather than "Roman Catholic" will be used through most of the book.

11

are valid from those that are invalid and destructive, and to encourage him to think realistically about them. Only by so doing can we hope to deal adequately with these problems.

Before the reader has finished the first chapter, it will be apparent that those whose views appear herein are hardly in agreement on what either the sources or the solutions of these tensions are. It will be suggested by some that the source lies in a monolithic, hierarchical church structure; by others that it results from social conditioning, or a failure of Protestants to realize and accept the proposition that this is no longer a Protestant country, or ignorance growing from a lack of dialogue and open discussion, etc.

Too frequently in general discussions of Protestant-Catholic tensions there is the implicit, if not explicit, expectation of both sides that the other will change. Protestants are expected to return to Rome; Catholics, on the other hand, are expected to give up doctrines basic to their faith and, in essence, become Protestants. Tensions can only be increased in such an atmosphere where conversion rather than conversation becomes the goal.

Since this book is concerned with helping the reader to deal with these tensions in a positive way, it is not concerned with conversion in either direction. It is concerned instead with a realistic assessment of these two dominant Christian groups by one another. I think it will be obvious to the reader that there is here no pulling of punches; there is an effort made both to know the truth and to speak one's own personal apprehension of that truth. Since truth is invariably apprehended differently, disagreements will continue. Nevertheless, tensions will be less destructive and will deal with more essential matters to the degree that real conversation and dialogue are achieved.

Brought together for the first time here in this volume are a series of essays that originally appeared in the pages of the Protestant fortnightly, *Christianity and Crisis*. These essays comprise all or the major portion of each chapter with the exception of Chapter VI. Chapters I, IV, and V include, in addition to the original essays, responses evoked at the time of their original appearance. In all cases both the articles and responses appear virtually as in the original; in most cases only those editorial changes that were required to fit them into the present volume were made.

There is considerable significance in the fact that both the essays and the responses appear together here. Anyone reading through the book cannot but be impressed by the attempt of all concerned to be as frank and honest as possible, at times excruciatingly so. No other volume with which I am acquainted has included as much "openness" as will be found here. The significance of this volume, it seems to me, lies equally as much in this fact as it does in the merit of the essays themselves.

The person who approaches this book with certain stereotypes that do not permit any re-examination of established thought patterns will be wasting his time. Those persons who are open to a fresh approach, who are willing to examine long held assumptions and prejudices in the hope of easing tensions—for these, this book offers insights to questions old and new. Clear and easy answers will not be forthcoming here, but the stimulus to continue the search for helpful ways of dealing with these tensions is offered in these thought-provoking pages.

I would like to express my gratitude to those persons whose articles comprise this volume, for their contribution to the developing conversation between Protestants and Catholics will be far-reaching; also to the Editorial Board of *Christianity and Crisis* for their encouragement in the undertaking of this project and their persistent belief in its worth; to Dr. John C. Bennett for his guidance and judgment at many points along the way; and especially to Mrs. Robert M. Hemings for her cheerful assistance in typing and preparing the manuscript.

WAYNE H. COWAN

ABOUT THE AUTHORS

A leader in Protestant thinking on the problems of the pluralist society, JOHN C. BENNETT is Dean of Union Theological Seminary in New York City, where he also teaches Christian ethics. Dr. Bennett's latest book in this area is the much appreciated *Christians and the State* (Scribner). One of the founders of *Christianity and Crisis*, he now serves as co-chairman of the Editorial Board.

FATHER GUSTAVE WEIGEL has been a close observer of the Protestant scene for a number of years. He has given considerable attention to Protestant theology and to ecumenical problems, and his review of the first volume of Paul Tillich's *Systematic Theology* is considered one of the best written to date. A Jesuit, Father Weigel taught for six years at the Catholic University of Chile. He now teaches ecclesiology at Woodstock College in Woodstock, Maryland.

Until recently at the Fordham University Graduate School, THOMAS F. O'DEA is Professor of Sociology at the University of Utah. Dr. O'Dea set fellow Catholics in this country to thinking about themselves in 1958 with his *American Catholic Dilemma* (Sheed and Ward), which presented an analysis of the factors inhibiting the development of intellectual life among American Catholics.

WILLIAM CLANCY, a former editor of the noted Catholic weekly *The Commonweal,* is Editor of *Worldview,* a journal of religion and international affairs. A consultant to the Fund for the Republic's study of Religion in a Democratic Society, Mr. Clancy also serves as Education Director of The Church Peace Union, an interfaith organization with headquarters in New York City.

As a leader in the World Council of Churches and the International Missionary Council, HENRY P. VAN DUSEN has observed Catholicism in many countries. Dr. Van Dusen has been President of Union Theological Seminary in New York City since 1945. He is a member of the Editorial Board of *Christianity and Crisis* as well as a founder of the journal. His most recent book is *Spirit, Son and Father.*

ROBERT MCAFEE BROWN, a Presbyterian minister, is Auburn Professor of Systematic Theology and Philosophy of Religion at Union Theological Seminary in New York City. A member of the Editorial Board of *Christianity and Crisis,* he has written widely on Protestant-Catholic relations. Early in 1960 he accomplished a noteworthy feat when his "Rules for the Dialogue" was published simultaneously by both *The Christian Century* and *The Commonweal.*

C. STANLEY LOWELL is Associate Director of Protestants and Other Americans United for the Separation of Church and State. He also edits their monthly publication *Church and State.*

ROBERT L. SCHLAGER is minister of First Methodist Church, "The American Church," in Buenos Aires, Argentina.

MONSIGNOR FRANCIS J. LALLY is Editor of *The Pilot*, an official publication of the Archdiocese of Boston.

FATHER BERNARD P. DAUENHAUER is a priest at St. Raphael Church in New Orleans, Louisiana.

WAYNE H. COWAN, for three years a missionary of the Methodist Church in Japan, is Managing Editor of *Christianity and Crisis*. He edited *What the Christian Hopes For in Society*, also a Reflection Book, and has written for *The Commonweal, The Christian Century*, and other journals.

Professor Emeritus of Teachers College, Columbia University, F. ERNEST JOHNSON has led a most active "retired" life. Since 1954 Dr. Johnson has served as Chief Economic Consultant to the Department of Church and Economic Life of the National Council of Churches. He is a member of the Executive Committee of the Institute for Religious and Social Studies of the Jewish Theological Seminary of America, and is also a Protestant consultant to the Fund for the Republic's Study of Religion in a Democratic Society.

PAUL BLANSHARD is a widely known lecturer and author. His book *American Freedom and Catholic Power* has gained wide attention.

DANIEL CALLAHAN is Teaching Fellow in Roman Catholic Studies in the Divinity School of Harvard University.

FACING PROTESTANT —
ROMAN CATHOLIC TENSIONS

I.

A PROTESTANT LOOKS AT AMERICAN CATHOLICISM

John C. Bennett

———

The attitudes of Americans toward church-state relations depend in considerable measure on their attitude toward Roman Catholicism. The chief concern that lies back of the convictions of non-Catholics is the concern for religious liberty, and the chief threat to religious liberty is seen in the tremendous growth of Roman Catholicism as a cultural and political power in the United States.

There are two deep problems connected with Catholicism that must be emphasized at the outset of any discussion. One is the *dogmatic intolerance* that is itself a part of the Roman Catholic faith. This dogmatic intolerance need not lead to *civil intolerance*, but there is a tendency for it to do so just as was the case when it characterized the major Protestant bodies. This dogmatic intolerance becomes all the more difficult for non-Catholics when it is associated not only with distinctly religious dogma, but also with elements of natural law that are not accepted as divinely sanctioned moral demands by most non-Catholics. This is true of birth control, of some matters of medical ethics. It is true even of gambling under limited conditions, though this has to do not with a moral demand but with a moral permission! One symptom of the dogmatic intolerance that is most objectionable to non-Catholics is the strict Catholic regulation concerning the religion of the children of mixed marriages.

The other basic problem is the real tension between an authoritarian, centralized hierarchical church and the spirit of an open, pluralistic, democratic society. There is abundant evidence that Catholics in this country do sincerely believe in democracy and practice this belief, but I do not see how they themselves can deny that their polity poses a problem for democracy that is not posed by churches which make their decisions in regard to public policy by processes of open discussion in which both clergy and laymen share. The polity of the Episcopal Church does give bishops meeting separately a veto over many things, but it also gives the laity voting separately in the dioceses a veto over the choice of bishops. I mention this as an example of one of the more hierarchical forms of polity outside the Roman Catholic Church.

The Roman polity is itself a matter of faith and therefore religious liberty includes the liberty to preserve that type of polity. And if it is said that the papacy creates a problem of peculiar difficulty because it is from the point of view of the nation a "foreign power," the answer that Protestants should be able to accept is that the Church as Church is supranational and the religious liberty of all Christians includes their right to have relationships, suitable to their polity, with the universal Church.

American Protestants are troubled over far more than these abstract problems created by the Catholic faith and ecclesiastical structure. They resent much that is done by the Catholic Church in America and they fear greatly what may yet be done. The books by Paul Blanshard, especially his *American Freedom and Catholic Power* (Beacon Press, 1949), marshal many facts that both Catholics and Protestants should take seriously. It is unfortunate that Mr. Blanshard has presented his material in such a way as to confuse criticism of many particular applications of Catholic teaching with what seems to be an attack on the freedom of a church to have its own authoritarian structure as a matter of faith. Also, he writes not from a Protestant but from a secularist point of view, and thus sees no inherent problem in the relation of religion to public education. He is quite satisfied with the complete separation of school and religion. There is a tendency to exaggerate the monolithic character of world-wide Catholicism under papal direction, and Mr. Blanshard's projection upon the future of the indefinite threat of Catholic power to American democracy does not, it seems to me, do justice to the four considerations I will emphasize later. The book is the work of a very energetic and well-informed prosecutor and should be used as such.

*The general thesis of this article is that, while many
of these resentments and fears are justified, it is a
mistake to project them in indefinitely extended form
upon the future and to allow all of our thinking about
Catholicism and most of our thinking about church-
state relations to be controlled by them in that extended form.* After outlining the grounds for some
justified resentments and fears in this article, I will
deal with other facts about Catholic life that should
play a larger part than they do in Protestant attitudes
toward Catholicism.

The Catholic Church is not a majority church in the
country at large and, since immigration has been
greatly limited, its rate of growth has not been quite
as rapid as the rate of growth of the Protestant
churches. But its strength is distributed so as to give
it great majorities in some cities, and enormous political power and cultural influence in many states.
It is extremely difficult for Protestants and other non-
Catholics to live with Catholicism as the religion of a
large local majority. It has likewise been difficult in
the past for Catholics to live with Protestantism as the
religion of a large local majority.

The centralized organization and the absolute
claims of the Church enhance the difficulty, but Protestants must not forget that any small minority feels
pressure that arouses resentments and fears under
these circumstances. Part of the problem is a universal
human tendency that does not depend on a particular
ecclesiastical situation. However, it is the threat of
a local majority that leads non-Catholics to emphasize

the protections of religious liberty in the Federal Constitution. Catholics also have had occasion to appeal to these same protections, but today their chief desire is to establish a somewhat flexible interpretation of the First Amendment.

Non-Catholics have grounds for resenting the tendency of Catholics to use their power to impose Catholic ideas of natural law. They see it in the birth control legislation in Massachusetts and Connecticut; they see it in the Catholic pressure to remove welfare agencies that have birth control clinics from local community chests elsewhere; they see it in the Catholic objection to divorce laws that are much more flexible than the law of the Church; they see it in the attempts to have non-Catholic hospitals adopt the Catholic ideas of medical ethics in the field of obstetrics.

Non-Catholics have grounds for resenting and fearing the tendency of Catholics, when they have the power, to seek control of the public school system to bend it to Catholic purposes. Parochial schools could operate as safety valves for the public schools but this is often not the case. When Catholics dominate the public school boards they sometimes discriminate against non-Catholic teachers. In extreme cases that have been much publicized they have operated public schools as though they were parochial schools. Perhaps more serious in the long run is the tendency of Catholics in some places to oppose needed bond issues or appropriations for the public schools. This is not a surprising reaction to the double burden of education costs that they themselves bear, but it is very bad for education.

Non-Catholics have grounds for resenting and fearing Catholic boycotts of communications media, including the publishers of books, and boycotts of local merchants who have some connection with a policy that they oppose. Fear of Catholic boycott often operates as a reason for self-censorship. Newspapers are influenced by this fear and it is very difficult to get news published that may be unfavorable to the Catholic Church.

No one can criticize the Catholic Church or any other church for seeking to discipline the theater-going or the reading of its own constituency. Boycotting that consists only of this self-discipline within the Church may be unfortunate in some of its effects, but it is not open to objection in principle. It is the punitive boycott directed against all that a particular agency may do that interferes with the freedom of non-Catholics.

The desire of many Catholics to have the United States send a diplomatic representative to the Vatican has become a symbol to most Protestants of the many things that they resent in the use of Catholic power. This issue is confused because it is obvious that in the world at large the representation of a nation at the Vatican is not interpreted as a sign that the nation involved shows favoritism to the Catholic Church. Otherwise there would not be representatives from many non-Christian countries, from Britain which has a state church .that is not the Catholic Church, nor from France which is secularist and anti-clerical in its politics.

But it is only fair to recognize the fact that the very size of the Catholic Church in this country and the absence of any state church, the existence of which would prove that the Catholic Church is not the favored church, makes American Protestants feel that diplomatic representation at the Vatican is a great concession to one American church in contrast to others. American Protestants emphasize the fact that the Pope is the head of one American church rather than the fact that the Vatican is the center of a diplomatic service which, as a unique institution of the old world, cannot be grasped by the American logic governing church-state relations.

Though I do not believe that this issue is as important as most Protestant leaders have made it, I have come to see that the meaning of representation at the Vatican to American non-Catholics in view of the actual religious situation in this country is natural, and the fact that this meaning exists here is more important than the fact that it does not exist in Britain or in Japan, for there are objective reasons for the difference. Because of them I believe that diplomatic representation of the American government at the Vatican will inevitably be interpreted as unfair to non-Catholics in this country.

Having summarized the grounds for Protestant fears and resentments in the face of the growth of Catholic power, I would now like to call attention to four characteristics of Catholicism that are often neglected in American Protestant discussions of this subject.

The first of these characteristics is Roman Catholicism's great variations from culture to culture and from country to country. The vision of many Protestants of a monolithic Catholic Church, built somewhat on the lines of the Stalinist empire, that is controlled from the Vatican is very wide of the mark. Historically it has proved itself capable of adjustment to the greatest variety of cultural conditions instead of being one kind of religious ethos exported from Rome.

The difference between French Catholicism and Spanish Catholicism almost belongs to the study of comparative religion. Catholicism in western Europe is utterly different from Catholicism in Latin America. In Germany, France, Holland, Belgium, Switzerland, and England we see what Catholicism can be when it is religiously and culturally mature and when it has learned to live with strong Protestant and secularist competition. There is remarkable intellectual ferment in the Catholic Church in those countries. Catholic thinkers take considerable theological freedom and they are especially free in their thinking about political issues. There is a long standing effort to overcome the political and economic conservatism that has been the great handicap of the Church in reaching the working classes.

There is very much more discussion between Protestant and Catholic thinkers on a theological level in Europe than there is in this country. One interesting phenomenon is the fresh study of Luther and the

Reformation by Catholic scholars that has shattered the old Catholic stereotypes. American Catholicism differs from western European Catholicism in that it has no rich cultural background. It has a strong feeling of cultural inferiority to American Protestantism as well as to European Catholicism. Intellectual ferment is exactly what it lacks. The reasons for this are obvious as American Catholicism represents the tides of immigration that brought to this country millions of Europeans who had had few opportunities in their own countries.

Protestants as they view the development of Catholicism have good reason to assume that as it becomes more mature culturally and theologically it will have more flexibility of mind and that there will be greater tolerance and breadth in dealing with non-Catholics and with the public issues that concern Protestants most.

I should add here that Catholicism needs not only the kind of maturing that takes time in a new country, but it needs to have two other things. One is the strong competition from non-Catholic sources—Protestant, Jewish, secularist. It has had one or more of these types of competition in every one of the western European countries that I named. The worst thing that can happen to Catholicism is for it to have the religious monopoly to which it feels entitled because of its exclusive claims! Protestants, therefore, have a responsibility to confront Catholicism with a positive Protestant theology, and that is happening today in

many countries because of the recent theological re-
vival in Protestantism.

The other element that is very important in the
environment for the development of Catholicism
along the lines that I have suggested is the presence
of a liberal, democratic political tradition. This has
greatly modified Catholic political attitudes and it is
most fortunate that, under the stimulus of democracy,
Catholics can find the antecedents of democracy in
their own tradition, especially in the great Jesuit
political philosophers, such as Francisco Suarez, in the
sixteenth and seventeenth centuries. They also discover antecedents of democracy in Thomas Aquinas.

This combination of continuous encounter with
non-Catholics on a basis of political mutuality and
the influence of liberal democratic ideas enables
Catholics to avoid the *civil intolerance* that causes
most anxiety among Protestants.

A second characteristic of Roman Catholicism is
suggested by the fact that much of the Catholic aggressiveness that is most offensive to Protestants is
sociologically conditioned. It is a result of the sheer
energy that it has taken for Catholics to improve their
position in a new country and in an alien culture, and
it also reflects some social resentment for past dis-
abilities on the part of people who have won social
power.

We forget today the long and bitter history of
nativist anti-Catholicism, but the memories of it do
not die so easily among Catholics themselves.

Today changes are coming so rapidly and the economic, social, and cultural opportunities for Americans of many ethnic backgrounds are so much alike that we can expect to see the particular sociological reasons for Catholic aggressiveness become less important.

Paul Blanshard recognizes that there is some truth in this consideration. After describing the role of the Irish in American Catholicism, he says:

> This Irish dominance explains many of the characteristics of American Catholicism. The Irish hierarchy which rules the American Church is a "becoming" class. It represents the Irish people struggling up in a hostile environment, using the Roman system of authoritative power to compensate for an inner sense of insecurity which still seems to survive from the days when Irish Catholics were a despised immigrant minority. Boston is aggressively Catholic largely because it is aggressively Irish, and it is aggressively Irish because its people have not quite overcome their sense of being strangers in a hostile land.[1]

One of the most convincing pieces of evidence in favor of this judgment concerning the social dynamics of American Catholicism is found in Kenneth Underwood's study in depth of Protestant-Catholic relations in one city that has had a large Catholic majority for some decades. Professor Underwood re-

---

[1] *American Freedom and Catholic Power* (Beacon Press, 1958), p. 38.

ports on the attitudes of both laymen and clergy from various parishes in Holyoke, Massachusetts. He finds that it is the parishes made up of recent immigrants, who have not been much assimilated into American life, where the most intolerant attitudes are found. It is those parishes where the rigid ideas of the priests are most readily accepted by laymen. He says:

> The upper income, well educated Catholic lay-men are much less receptive to clerical guidance as to the practical social implications of moral and religious laws of the church than are the lower income, more poorly educated Catholics. The former tend also to be much more apprecia-tive of the rôle of the Protestant churches in supplementing or correcting Catholic action.[2]

A third fact about Catholicism that needs to be understood by Protestants is that the Catholic Church is divided from top to bottom, in this country and abroad, on matters of principle in regard to religious liberty. There is a traditional main-line position that favors the confessional Catholic state as the ideal type of relationship between church and state. This view would limit the rights of religious minorities in a nation that has a very large Catholic majority. These limitations would have to do with public propagation of the non-Catholic faith rather than with freedom of worship or freedom of teaching inside the Protestant

---

[2] *Protestant and Catholic* (Beacon Press, 1957) , p. 94.

Church. Under such circumstances there would be a union of state and church and the state as state would profess the Catholic faith.

This position is sometimes called the "thesis" and the adjustments of the Church to religiously pluralistic nations, including the acceptance by American Catholics of the American constitutional separation of church and state, involve a second-best position called the "hypothesis." Father John A. Ryan, a noted Catholic liberal on all economic issues, is responsible for a famous statement on this subject. He states the traditional thesis and then tries to soften it for Americans by saying:

> While all of this is very true in logic and in theory the event of its practical realization in any state or country is so remote in time and in probability that no practical man will let it disturb his equanimity or affect his attitude toward those who differ from him in religious faith.[3]

So long as Protestants, especially those who live in cities that already have large Catholic majorities, realize that there are authoritative statements of the so-called Catholic thesis of the confessional state as representing the ideal possibility, they will not be greatly comforted by Father Ryan's assurances. It is simply not enough for a church that operates in the

---

[3] J. Ryan and F. Boland, *Catholic Principles of Politics* (Macmillan, 1940), p. 320.

light of very clear dogmatic principles to make con-
cessions on the issue of religious liberty for non-
Catholics on a pragmatic basis alone if its dogmatic
principles still point to a confessional Catholic state
in which, as the ideal, the religious liberties of minorities are severely restricted.

It is important to realize that a very able and
earnest attempt is being made by Catholic scholars in
this country, with much support from Catholics in
western Europe, to change the principles as well as
the practice of the Church in this matter. This attempt
is associated chiefly with the work of Father John
Courtney Murray, but it is gaining a good deal of
support elsewhere too. A careful statement of his position is found chiefly in his many articles in the Jesuit
quarterly *Theological Studies*. (See especially March,
1953; June, 1953; December, 1953; March, 1954. Also,
"Governmental Repression of Heresy" reprinted from
the Proceedings of the Catholic Theological Society
of America.)

Here I shall attempt to summarize his main conclu-
sions, but it should be recognized that these are ab-
stracted from very complicated historical expositions
and come in large part from Father Murray's analysis
of the encyclicals of Pope Leo XIII in order to show
what is permanent and what is historically conditioned in those encyclicals. With apologies to Father
Murray for oversimplification of the kind that is alien
to his own mind, I shall attempt to give the substance
of his position in the following propositions:

The idea of a confessional Catholic state belongs

to an earlier period in European history and it has become an irrelevancy under contemporary conditions.

Anglo-Saxon democracy is fundamentally different from the democracy of the French Revolution which was totalitarian in tendency. The state in this country is, by its very nature, limited, and in principle the Church does not need to defend itself against such a state as it did with the nineteenth century revolutionary states that formed the immediate background of Leo's political thinking.

There is no anti-clerical or anti-religious motivation behind the American constitutional provision for church-state relations and the Church need not defend herself against this doctrine as such.

The Church in America has, as a matter of fact, enjoyed greater freedom and scope for its witness and activities than it has in the Catholic states of the traditional type.

It is important to emphasize the rights of the state in its own sphere, the freedom of the Church from state control, and the influence of Catholic citizens upon the state.

It is impossible to separate religious freedom from civil freedom, and there can be no democracy if the freedom of the citizen is curtailed in religious matters, for such curtailing can often take place as a means of silencing political dissent.

Error does not have the same rights as truth, but persons in error, consciences in error, do have rights that should be respected by the Church and state.

The Church should not demand that the state as the secular arm enforce the Church's own decisions in regard to heresy.

It does more harm than good to the Church for the state to use its power against non-Catholics.

I think that all of these propositions fit together into a self-consistent social philosophy. They are presented by Father Murray as a substitute for the traditional Catholic thesis concerning the confessional state. They have made considerable headway among both clergy and laity in this country. They correspond to views that are held in Europe and have support in the Vatican itself.

In December, 1953, after this point of view was strongly rebuked by Cardinal Ottaviani in Rome in an address defending the Spanish conception of a confessional Catholic state as the ideal, Pope Pius XII somewhat ambiguously made room for Murray's position in a speech to a convention of Catholic jurists. The fact that he did this in the midst of a trans-Atlantic controversy within the Church has encouraged American Catholics who hold this view to believe that the Pope was sympathetic to it. That is the most that can be said.

American Protestants should realize, therefore, that the Roman Church is not a vast international machine designed to overturn their liberties, if this were to become politically possible, and that they have many allies in the Catholic Church who share their belief in religious liberty on principle.

The fourth fact about the Catholic Church is that there are many points of disagreement on social policy among Catholics; there is no one Catholic line on most public issues. There is agreement on birth control as a moral issue, but even here there is no agreement as to what the state should do about it. Catholics generally do not today advocate strict laws on the subject except in the two states in which those laws are already in force. On economic issues there is a broad Catholic pattern based upon the organization of producers' groups, but this is far from obligatory and it gives rise to endless differences so far as application is concerned.

Catholics differ as to whether a war with modern weapons can be just. There is a deep difference between Catholics in various nations on forms of government. Catholic doctrine makes room for governments based upon popular sovereignty but does not prescribe this universally. Even on communism there are great differences in temper between European and much American Catholicism.

It is an understatement to say that the Catholic hierarchy did not act helpfully on the issue of McCarthyism, but that was because they were deeply divided. There is no doubt that McCarthy had a strong hold on large groups of Catholics, especially Irish Catholics, but it is also true that some of the most eloquent opposition to McCarthy came from Catholic sources, notably such journals as *The Commonweal* and *America*. American Protestants need not fear that Catholics will usually throw their great weight as a religious community in the same political direction. This will tend to be even less a danger as Catholics move further away from the status of an immigrant bloc. In general we can say that natural law does not guarantee agreement on concrete issues, but we can also say that natural law plus prudence equals flexibility.

I have outlined briefly four aspects of Catholicism of which American Protestants should take account. Though they give no assurance as to the direction that Catholicism may take in the next generation, they may release us from exaggerated fears based on past experience in this country alone. Protestants should put more rather than less emphasis upon positive elements of Protestant faith and doctrine. They should join Catholics in rejecting superficial forms of religious harmony so often urged in the interests of national unity. But they can live with their Catholic neighbors in the hope that greater mutual understanding and the sharing of moral and political purposes may become possible.

• Salient Facts Overlooked

*A Concerned Protestant Suggests Another View
of Catholic Religious Liberty*

C. STANLEY LOWELL

It impresses me that in his "argument from difference" in regard to Catholic views on religious liberty,

John Bennett overlooks some salient facts. He fails to mention that while the "American view" of Father Murray was being advanced against the traditional Catholic view of religious liberty pressed by the Spanish hierarchy, Cardinal Ottaviani's statement settling the issue was approved by the Pope as "unexceptionable." Nor does he mention that Cardinal Ottaviani, as Secretary of the Supreme Congregation of the Holy Office, was perhaps the Pope's closest confidant.

Dr. Bennett does make vague mention of a speech in which the Pope, himself in vague language, seems to lend some approval to "the American view." If any such pronouncement exists, it must appear rather emaciated when contrasted with the overwhelming evidence of pronouncements on the other side.

While it is nice that Father Murray holds "liberal views," the fact is that they have never gained any official recognition at the Vatican. Unfortunately, Father Murray speaks for no one, not even himself. Authoritative teaching of the American hierarchy in regard to religious liberty, a teaching squarely in line with the Church's tradition, has been consistently presented by Father Francis J. Connell.

It seems curious, too, that Dr. Bennett should speak of "the influence of liberal democratic ideas [which] enables Catholics to avoid the civil intolerance that causes most anxiety among Protestants." He apparently wrote this at the very moment that New York was in an uproar over a sectarian medical code that the Roman Catholic Church had for years been imposing on public hospitals of that city.

• Reply to Mr. Lowell

JOHN C. BENNETT

Mr. Lowell raises an important question. How influential in the Catholic Church is the view of Father Murray that was outlined in my article? I emphasized the fact that it is not the dominant view. It has the tradition of many centuries against it. The most that I can claim is that this issue of the religious liberty of non-Catholics in a nation in which there is a predominance of Catholics is being debated on all levels and in many countries, and that the traditional position is being challenged with great ability. The so-called "dynamic interpreters," to use the name given by Father Gustave Weigel to the Murray position, have strong support among Catholic scholars and laymen in this country and in several other democratic countries.

Professor Kenneth Underwood, in *Protestant and Catholic,* points out that in Holyoke, Mass., 40 per cent of the clergy, and these the younger clergy, are receptive to this position (pp. 352–53). One difficulty is that, without raising the ultimate question of the theory of religious liberty, Catholics in this country can agree with the practical implications of Father Murray's position on pragmatic grounds. Members of the hierarchy do not want to be put on the spot on a matter that involves revision of basic theory. The discussion is being carried out by scholars and laymen.

The speech by Cardinal Ottaviani actually revealed the division within the Church because he was strongly attacked publicly by Catholic spokesmen in this country, even by such a diocesan journal as *The Pilot* in Boston. I have learned by word of mouth about the serious divisions in the Vatican concerning this speech, but this quickly becomes gossip and it is hard to evaluate. Pius XII's address to which I referred (distributed in English translation on December 15, 1953) did not go further than the traditional position allows, but the timing of it suggests that he was in fact rebuking the extreme position advanced by Cardinal Ottaviani. The address itself shows the caution and even studied ambiguity that are common in papal utterances. The most that we can expect of any Pope on such matters is an indication of permissiveness. Remember that we are dealing here with a theoretical challenge of the traditional position; but this challenge has great significance because it fits the experience of Catholics in democratic countries. Elsewhere Pius XII made a very clear place for democracy.

As far as birth control is concerned, I agree with those who fight uncompromisingly for the freedom of non-Catholics on this issue. There are important issues between Protestants and Catholics and I do not want to obscure them. Fortunately there is some disagreement among Catholics as to how far they

should press their position on the whole community
by law. There is a favorable straw in the wind in the
fact that they are not attempting to have laws such as
those in Massachusetts and Connecticut enacted in
other states. But if this means that they are relying on
administrative action, as was the case in New York
City hospitals, they need to be resolutely opposed.

• Complex and Evolving Realities

*An Irritated Catholic Insists That the Roman
Church Is a Living, Changing Institution*

William Clancy

It is depressing to read the observations of C.
Stanley Lowell. They give further evidence of remarkable inability even to glimpse the realities of
Catholicism in the modern world. These realities, as
John C. Bennett has observed, are complex and, in
many areas, evolving. But, whatever may be the evidence to the contrary, Mr. Lowell insists that "the
Roman Church" is simple and forever frozen in some
medieval mold.

I am not hopeful that anything I, or any other
Catholic, might say would bring him to a wider vision
of Catholicism. Those who see it as authoritarianism
pure and simple, a monolithic conspiracy against the
"American way of life," are frozen in *their* mold. But
for the sake of those Protestants and others who are

interested, I think some Catholic comment should be made.

The point I would make is general. But I must also point out several of his more outrageous inaccuracies.

Item: Mr. Lowell claims that Cardinal Ottaviani's 1953 defense of the "traditional" Catholic church-state position was "approved" by the Pope as "unexceptionable." He further states that "if" (as Dr. Bennett wrote) the Pope once made a speech which "in vague language seems to approve 'the American view,' " the Pope's pronouncement, "if any such pronouncement exists . . . must appear rather emaciated when contrasted with the overwhelming evidence of pronouncements on the other side."

These are startling observations. The late Pope himself never made *any* comment on Cardinal Ottaviani's address. Someone in "the Vatican," who has never been identified, made a statement that while the Ottaviani position was "*neither official nor semi-official*" it was, nevertheless, "unexceptionable." And the "vague" papal pronouncement that Mr. Lowell seems to doubt was ever made was, in fact, a major— some think historic—allocution, delivered in 1953 to an audience of Italian jurists, in which Pope Pius XII laid down the principle that "in the interest of a higher and broader good, it is justifiable not to impede error by state laws and coercive measures." It remains true, Pius declared, that error has no rights "objectively," but "the duty to repress religious and moral deviation cannot be an ultimate norm for action. It must be subjected to higher and more general norms." Many Catholics in the West interpreted this principle, clearly stated by the Pope, as "officially" opening the way for the formulation of a new Catholic position on church-state relations.

Item: Mr. Lowell believes that "while it is nice [*sic*] that Father John Courtney Murray holds 'liberal views,' the fact is that they have never gained any official recognition at the Vatican. Unfortunately, Father Murray speaks for no one, not even himself."

Comment on this seems unnecessary in view of Pius XII's pronouncement to the Italian jurists. One can only observe that it would be "nice" if Mr. Lowell had paid at least as much attention to the official papal address that undercut his view of Catholicism as he did to "the neither official nor semi-official" speech that supported it.

But of course he did not. And here we see the reason why most Catholics despair of any rational discussion with those who hold his views, particularly with supporters of Protestants and Other Americans United. As I observed before, they will *insist* that the Catholic Church is a simple, forever frozen authoritarian phenomenon, incapable of historic adaptation or self-criticism, no matter how impressive the evidence to the contrary may be. The historic ferment and developments in modern Catholic thought are dismissed (if anything is known about them) as atypical or even hypocritical. For how could it be otherwise in a Church that is "monolithic"? Period.

. . . But though the Church has a life that is beyond

history, it also moves in history and here it learns, adapts, changes. It is not the simple, mechanical "power" that some of its critics fear. The Church is living, not dead.

At the beginning of this century a great Roman Pontiff, Leo XIII, wrote: "It is the special property of human institutions and laws that there is nothing in them so holy and salutary but that custom may alter it, or overthrow it, or social habits bring it to naught. So in the Church of God, in which change-ableness of discipline is joined with absolute im-mutability of doctrine, it happens not rarely that things which were once relevant or suitable become in the course of time out of date, or useless, or even harmful."

Here was as "official" an observation as any Mr. Lowell could desire. And, in its spirit, the process of separating out those things that are essential from those that are unessential, of re-evaluating those things which, in the course of time, may have become useless or even harmful, will continue in the Catholic community during the reign of John XXIII. While it proceeds, Catholics will hope for patience and some intelligent understanding from those not of the house-hold of their faith.

II.

AMERICAN CATHOLICISM ASSESSED FROM WITHIN

GUSTAVE WEIGEL, S.J.

———

An editor of a Protestant journal of opinion recently stated that one of the current tasks facing a Protestant religious journalist is to tell American Protestants that America is no longer a Protestant country. Whether Protestants have to be informed of this fact may possibly be debated but the fact itself cannot be. Yet no one will draw the illegitimate conclusion that America is already or is becoming a Catholic land. Percentage-wise, the Catholic Church has not grown much in the last forty years.

But in this land of many religious minorities how are we to interpret the Catholic reality? Sociological studies have been made but the limitations and detachment with which such studies are produced rarely shed great light on the lived existence of the Catholic collectivity. An investigation must be made from the inside. Yet this is a difficult task. There certainly is something that can be called a collective consciousness of the total group, but to get at it one must rely on an individual consciousness that is hopelessly hemmed in by its own individuality. Nevertheless, it is worth while to make an attempt at investigation even under such precarious conditions.

Aristotle wanted definitions to be derived from genus and differentiae. The American Catholic Church is therefore a Catholic church and different from all other Catholic churches because it is American. This may seem to say little, but actually it says much. Differences are not accidentals tacked on to the genus. They suffuse it totally.

There is no call here to describe generic Catholicism. Our effort will be directed to the American differentiae. The American component of American Catholicism obviously entered into it by way of history. Into a land staked off as the claim of Protestant groups, the Catholic intruded. This intrusion came not as a single blow but in a steady flow over 150 years. By and large the Catholic came either as a non-English speaker or as an Irishman. In either case he was culturally alien to the British possessors of the land. Religiously he was not only different but suspect.

Whether we like it or not, Protestants and Catholics are inevitably related to each other by the concept of opposition, and the opposition is stronger the nearer we approach the moment of the split of one from the other. Today we are all striving manfully to overcome the sense of opposition, but we are descendants of the past and history works in all of us.

The first Catholics, therefore, walked into a hostile

environment. This does not mean that there were barbarous persecutions or gross inhumanity. The persecutions were petty and the individual Catholic could and did avoid them either through personal friendship with individual Protestants or by taking refuge in a ghetto built by himself and his kind.

The immigrating Catholics were also, in general, poor folk escaping from the hardships proper to lower social classes of Europe. They did not bring with them much learning, nor even a great awareness of the good of learning. The capital the Catholic brought with him was his will to improve his secular condition and his readiness to work hard in his attempts. Those who did not have this capital returned to their lands of origin or soon died.

As the English know, America, in spite of its English roots, is not England. It is a new thing with subtle power. The American Dream, or whatever we wish to call it, had (and pray God that it still has!) a transforming power that it infused into its own, making them one. The European Catholics who came to America became American. The result was that the Catholicism they brought with them became American as well.

It was not done without growing pains. Some of the Europeans of the nineteenth century did not want an American Catholic Church but a confederation of European Catholic churches on American soil. They were led by German spokesmen, but World War I showed the Americans of German stock that they themselves were Americans and not Germans. The whole American Catholic Church suddenly became aware of itself as Catholic and American and has never since lost that awareness.

From 1918 onwards, Catholicism in America took on a new vitality because of its own achieved identification. The result was that any clear-eyed observer could see that the American Catholic Church was a power and a force in the land. It was no longer struggling to survive or to be accepted. It had "arrived."

However, the effects of its earlier history showed up clearly. There was a sudden pride of achievement that was more adolescent than mature. Catholicism became cocky and would tolerate no criticism from within or without. Where it could, it "threw its weight around." The older fear and resentment toward Protestants now turned into smug, but edgy, aloofness. One could almost hear the American Catholics say: "You have had your day; now we have ours."

The pain and distress involved in the Al Smith campaign of 1928 was a salutary and chastening experience. Even if America was not religiously Protestant, it was by no means pro-Catholic. In consequence, a more objective self-examination slowly spread over the group. Catholics began to criticize themselves and did so with a candor that should have amazed non-Catholics—but they did not even notice.

The basic weakness inherent in the Catholic community was its lack of scholarship. It had loyalty, organization, and numerical strength but it had too little intellectualism, in spite of its growing educational system built laboriously by the Catholics without outside aid. This weakness could not become conscious until a sufficient number of American Catholic intellectuals were formed; and they were being formed in the '30s and '40s. The result is that voices have been since heard and embarrassment felt. However, these things are themselves the first steps of coming improvement.

At the present moment, the American Catholic Church is neither a harassed minority nor a belligerent group. It is more prone to conservatism than radical change. Its tendency is toward American chauvinism rather than anything anti-American. It is rather contemptuous of what is foreign, even when visible in the Catholic Church elsewhere. Its generosity, activism, and optimism are probably more American than Catholic.

One thing American Protestants must recognize, though they are slow to do so, is that American Catholics are no threat to them, nor do they wish to be. The diminution of Protestant power understandably makes Protestants nervous, but there is no ground in Catholicism for their nervousness.

The American Catholics do not consider Protestantism as their great preoccupation nor do they pay much attention to it. They arrange their own affairs and conversations with little or no concern for the Protestant dimension of our country. At times they are faced with certain movements that have a nuisance value, as for example the Protestants and Other Americans United for Separation of Church and State

(POAU), that Catholics fortunately do not identify with the Protestant community. (In fact, it must be embarrassing for many Protestants to see this group use in its proper name a label that is so much bigger than it and that means something better than the POAU movement.) However, in general the American Catholics do not define themselves or their activities in terms of Protestant reference.

This attitude, besides the advantage of eliminating maintained hostility for Protestantism, also has a palpable disadvantage. Although American Catholics have many friends and relatives who are Protestants, yet they know so little about Protestantism and show no great desire to know more. It would almost be true to say that the American Catholics, in constant amicable relationships with Protestants, ignore Protestantism. They are not curious to find out the doctrines of Protestantism, nor its ways of worship and structure. It is not clear in their minds what distinguishes an Episcopalian from a Methodist. Luther vaguely means something, but Lutherans are supposed to be undifferentiated Protestants with a German background. The multitude of the more angular, smaller denominations simply confuses the Catholic without stimulating him to clarify his confusion.

In such a situation the American Catholic is totally unprepared for ecumenical dialogue, though this is the task that our moment calls for. There is no Catholic hostility to ecumenism. There just a great ignorance of what it is and why it is important.

Some few voices have been raised in American

Catholic circles pointing sympathetically to the ecumenical movement, and they have been heard. But they have not made a deep or wide impact. Perhaps the few Catholic ecumenists will manage to arouse great interest in their work, and there are signs that the young Catholics, clerical and lay, are waking up to its importance. However, as of the moment not much is being accomplished. The American Catholic makes his own the principle lately enunciated by Professor Oscar Cullmann—that Catholicism and Protestantism are irreconcilable. But unlike Cullmann, the American Catholic does not see that much must yet be done in Christian charity.

The electoral campaign of 1960 is already aborning. The presence of Senator John Kennedy among the possible candidates will produce intranquillity. In God's goodness it may be the occasion for Catholic ecumenical action. Perhaps it may even do the contrary.

Certainly the ecumenical council to be summoned by Pope John XXIII should produce some good fruits, at least in the world-wide preparations for the council sessions. Just now, with these possibilities before us, we must wait, hope, and see.

III.

THE MISSING DIALOGUE

Thomas F. O'Dea

Oscar Cullmann stated recently that the prerequisite for Protestant-Catholic conversation is "complete openness." Actually this aim, achievable among some groups in Europe, is too high for American conditions. The best we can do is to work for a growing openness as we build some basis in mutual trust and friendship. Our bridges are very weak. They bear a warning—"Capacity: not too many tons"—and we are all quite good at implicitly reading such signs.

Thus, Protestant-Catholic dialogue in this country does not take place in an atmosphere of relaxation and interior freedom. It is usually characterized by a kind of distant and respectful restraint expressing a kind of etiolated good will. Only real and fairly continuous association can bring relaxation of such attitudes. While individuals achieve this, representative individuals in religious or semi-religious dialogue usually fall far short of it. And the two great religious bodies certainly do not attain anything like this.

One result of this general absence of Christian dialogue is that one receives the impression—rather a caricature of the facts—that the reciprocal attitudes of the two groups are quite antagonistic. This impression arises from the statements and actions of the noisier elements on each side, who may be characterized loosely in terms of two identifiable groups.

Let us call them, for want of better terms, Catholic hyper-integralists and Protestant hyper-reformationists. Both find a marked satisfaction in carrying out, quite inappropriately in the contemporary setting, religious conflicts of the past. The source of this satisfaction deserves deep study. All that can be done here is to suggest some elements that must be included in any adequate hypothesis.

The Catholic hyper-integralists want two incompatible things at once. They want some kind of Catholic ghetto and, at the same time, they seek to identify Catholicism with America and Americanism, understanding the latter especially in terms of right-wing political opinions. They see no need for any larger expression of Christian solidarity nor any useful end in genuine dialogue with Protestants or others about fundamental value-problems. Their viewpoint is an ideology in the sense that it displays a marked economy in relation to the ambiguities of reality. It is a set of stereotypes and is given to blacks and whites, rights and wrongs, fors and againsts.

Ideologies are embraced because they serve some function—often implicit and unrecognized—for their adherents. They fulfill needs and allay anxieties.

Hyper-integralists suffer from two strains, both derived from their historical experience. They experience the defensiveness of all Christianity before the rapid secularization of culture. This is aggravated by the defensive posture that much of post-Tridentine Catholicism has inherited from the Counter Reformation.

Another closely related set of strains derives from the American Catholic experience. Immigration and assimilation were difficult processes for those involved, and they precipitated attitudes that did not simply fade away when the most palpable difficulties no longer existed. Catholics were not well received at first. This is a fact, one that Protestants perhaps do not ponder enough. Many of them were Irish and brought with them bitter memories of oppression by a Protestant ruling class in Ireland. Thus certain symbols and their attendant feeling tones are often differently experienced by Catholics and Protestants, who in fact may be equally "democratic."

Consequently Catholics as a group have developed a complex relationship to America, and the complexity lies precisely in areas not easily understood by the ordinary man. The American Catholic feels himself an American, wants to be and is glad he is an American, takes over American middle-class values and joins the social mobility merry-go-round alongside his Protestant fellows.

To the extent that he remains Catholic, he often finds it difficult to relate himself to some aspects of American culture, especially to intellectual areas of life that derive from a Protestant substrate and show pronounced secularization, and to other areas more closely related to Protestantism proper.

When Catholics become middle class they take over many of the general fears and anxieties of the middle class, fears of aggrandizement of other groups at their expense. Since Catholics derived recently from lower-class status, their new middle-class attitudes may involve some degree of guilt.

Moreover, since Catholic values have stressed social ethics, the new political and social attitudes may involve guilt on this score. The unevenly assimilated Catholic needs something to enable him to handle these problems, something to give him a new conception and legitimation of himself and to supply him with the basic security that is derived in less mobile societies from social solidarity and tradition. This function is served by the ideology of hyper-integralism.

This is done by making a strident identification of Catholicism with America and Americanism, which also exorcises the heritage of the Enlightenment and its modern leftist derivatives. Not only is Catholicism equated with genuine Americanism, but secularism is rendered un-American, and criticism of bourgeois values becomes anti-American and anti-Catholic. America, the business system, and the Catholic Church stand together, attacked by a common enemy. Their defense is a single task.

The earlier defensiveness invites a militant response and the bothersome problems—difficult to make explicit and to evaluate rationally—are translated into bogeys to be combatted. Thus a lot of anxiety-provoking problems are given some kind of formulation, and therapists tell us that any kind of definition offers a measure of relief. Furthermore, identification of the problems makes an attack upon them possible, albeit only a symbolic one. But the symbolic attack provides the self-definition that is needed and acts as a catharsis for built-up tensions.

Three marks of ideology may be distinguished: stereotyped oversimplification of reality, militancy, and rigidity. The last reveals the presence of anxiety, and the presence of aggressiveness is an obvious response to strain. We have here a historically conditioned social and cultural syndrome involving displacement and projection. I do not mean that it is a neurosis in the individual sense, though in some cases it may be. It is an instance of social pathology.

The hyper-reformationists—the Protestant equivalents of the Catholics just described—also react in terms of historical conditioning to contemporary strains. Protestants and Protestantism today are having to accept something less than the central and dominant position they have long had in American culture and society. The social mobility of other groups, among whom the Catholics are prominent, makes this the case.

Once securely identified with the core of American culture and society, Protestants now must move over a bit. That men do not move over graciously is one of the few undeniable generalizations from history. This adjustment is not yet clearly explicit in Protestant thinking, but the nudge is felt and is responded to.

When upsetting social developments, such as industrialization and urbanization, shook American society in the nineteenth century, it was fairly standard for many Protestant groups to respond in terms of anti-Catholic clichés. The great and honorable tradition of Protest has had the unfortunate by-product of supplying the man in the street with a ready set of counters from Foxe's *Martyrs* and the "Black Legend" with which to organize experience. Such clichés serve similar purposes today.

Catholics are certainly nervous in the face of the rapid secularization of culture, but Protestants are, often enough, inundated by it. A curious aspect of this development, which does not aid the inner security of Protestant church groups, is that some secularized Protestants tend to identify Catholicism with the older orthodox tradition of Christianity, something certainly in no way encouraged by official Protestantism. When such people feel guilt—often not very consciously—for no longer believing what they were brought up to believe, they tend to project it outwards and to aggress Catholicism as the external visible surrogate of their former beliefs.

The hyper-reformationists see as their chief religious and civic task the carrying forward of the counter-Catholic aspects of the Reformation in today's world. In fact, the very weakening of their Protestantism by secularization makes them more and not less anti-Catholic for the reasons I have suggested, and also because it is the one aspect of the long and honorable tradition of the Reformation that is meaningful to them in their present situation.

More pressing problems such as the very problematic future of all religion in American culture do not bother them despite their close relation to rational Protestant interests. By saving America from "Catholic aggression," this ideology once again identifies Protestantism with America and symbolically reaffirms the older, central role of Protestantism in our society.

This is, in fact, a symbolic counterattack against the social rise of Catholics and the inevitably concomitant increasing visibility and influence of Catholicism. In some cases at least, it is also a way of handling guilt over an older, abandoned Protestant orthodoxy. This ideology, too, shows itself as employing a truncating stereotyping and as exhibiting militancy and rigidity. Like its Catholic counterpart, it goes in heavily for verbal realism.

Some will object that there is certainly some truth in what hyper-reformationism says about "Catholic authoritarianism," or in what hyper-integralism says about liberalism and Protestant "connivance" with secularism. Yes, of course. If they were not built upon some reality, ideologies would not serve their function. The real bases exist in the complicated social developments we have briefly indicated and in the real and important faith and value differences that exist between Catholics and Protestants.

The neurotic individual who reacts to his boss in terms of unsolved infantile problems in relation to his father does not imagine that his boss is an authority figure who creates problems for him. This is part of the real situation. What he does is to perceive this realistic element in a context derived from earlier and now inappropriate experiences. He adds unreal elements. In part he does this by schematizing the current situation in terms of the dimension of the earlier one. The perception is a distorted one and the reaction is overdetermined. In the same way, these ideologists respond to their present predicaments with older and now inappropriate organizing ideas and actions. In both cases this is a disguised way of handling anxieties, wishes, and aggressions.

These ideologies provide for each group a simplified and manageable definition of the situations in which they find themselves. They provide the self-image needed in a time of rapid transition to replace the older conventional images and definitions now being rendered obsolete by social change. The plight of the individual in a progressively complicated society also finds some fantasy expression as do frustrations and aggressions of more purely personal origin.

It should be stressed that the anti-Romanism of the one and the anti-liberalism of the other are the sociological equivalents of the anti-Semitism of the German conservative classes who proved so vulnerable to Nazism. Why these ideologies appeal only to some elements among both religious groups and not to all is deserving of serious research. Undoubtedly some groups are more securely anchored in reality.

There are three reasons why I have considered at length these groups that are not representative of the typical Catholic or Protestant. First, they should not be underestimated; they are not a lunatic fringe. There are hard cores on both sides, and around them cluster all shades of affected opinion.

Second, these groups should be a problem to intelligent Catholics and Protestants. It is important that they do not come to act as foci for the crystallization of American opinion.

Third, these ideologies play an important part in structuring the framework in which a great deal of exchange of ideas takes place. The exchanges are often marked by considerable intensity. Issues like education, birth control, an ambassador to the Vatican, or a Catholic President arouse the hyper-reformationists.

Their Catholic counterparts are in fact likely to remain calmer and more rational on these issues, which they see more realistically and less symbolically. They tend to get triggered off by such symbolic counters as communism, which plays the role of master-symbol for many of them, criticism of the F.B.I., or Alger Hiss speaking at Princeton, over which a Catholic chaplain becomes so exercised. Some symbols are shared in common, and in local contexts any of the long list may become the catalyst to set things off.

Fortunately, these two ideologies are not organized around the same symbols, and their adherents do not face each other as two quite polarized groups reacting with equal intensity to the same issues. The loosely integrated character of American society and culture helps account for this fact.

It is ironical that neither group seems aware that both constitute striking examples of the secularization of their religious ethos. If the hyper-integralists see no inconsistency in championing a Catholicism that has centered its ethic upon *caritas* ("charity," cf. I Cor. 13) and, at the same time, in embracing Joseph McCarthy as a sterling defender of the cause, the hyper-reformationists see nothing anti-Protestant in the crude secularism of Paul Blanshard on so many ethical issues. Each confuses religion and secular nationalism in its own way.

Thus the hyper-integralists tend to merge loosely into rightist secular political groupings, a fact that reaffirms their Americanism for them. The hyper-reformationists also merge loosely, in some cases at least, with quite militant secularizers.

Certain conservative Protestant groups today appear to be taking up a line like the hyper-integralists. As recent events in the South have shown, the identification of conservative and defensive religion with right-wing causes is not a Catholic monopoly. Will the hyper-reformationists reconcile themselves with their Catholic equivalents on the basis of a secular rightism and find themselves combating fellow Protestants?

An important effect of the existence of these ideologies is, as I have noted, that they tend to define
the universe of discourse for more moderate people.
The result is a great lack of reality-testing about
controversial issues. To give but one example: it is
surprising to what a great extent the discussion of a
possible Catholic President is marked by tenseness
and lack of sense of proportion. The symbolic elements outweigh the real in the thinking of so many
otherwise sensible people.

It seems clear to any political realist that no Catholic President would or could alter the American
Constitution, either as a document or as a body of
practices embodying and interpreting that document.
Certainly this is one area where formal and informal
control seems quite effective.

Indeed, anyone with an ounce of political shrewdness knows that the Catholic Church as a religious
group would have far less influence upon a Catholic
President than upon almost any other conceivable
administration. The social controls are such that he
would lean over backwards to avoid even the suggestion of influence. In France members of the clergy
were much freer in approaching high government
officials under distinctly secular cabinets than they
were when MRP, a liberal Catholic party, had formed
the government.

Every issue of this kind picks up connotations that
find resonance in Catholic and Protestant souls, re-
activating memories of our unfortunate and most
unchristian history of fighting and persecuting one

another—triggering off our often unconscious and, too often, equally unchristian anxieties about our present predicaments. These foreshortened attempts to handle a reality we have not really faced are in fact an unwary abandonment of reality. Non-rational fears and aggressions replace Christian action: symbolic concerns replace real ones.

Reality-testing must be developed, but reality-testing is not an individual process. It is a social affair in which the slants of men with different perspectives partly correct and partly supplement each other, eliminating fantasy and enlarging the range of the real. It requires communication, the basis of which should exist in a common Christian heritage.

In isolation, each group finds it difficult to recognize in its own view the elements of fantasy and projection that creep in. That is why Protestant-Catholic dialogue is so important. It has already started in theological discussions and in biblical studies. There is much room for creative thinking in extending it. Only dialogue will deliver us from the spell of the ideologists.

IV.

HOW AMERICAN PROTESTANTISM LOOKS TO A ROMAN CATHOLIC

WILLIAM CLANCY

If there be *a* Christian commandment, it is surely the commandment of love. "By this," Jesus told us, "will all men know that you are my disciples, if you love one another." But if the standard of this commandment were strictly applied, we would find few "Christians" in any age. As for the situation in America today, Reinhold Niebuhr has accurately observed: "The relations between Catholics and Protestants in this country are a scandal and an offense against Christian charity."

The scandal of our Protestant-Catholic relations may, of course, be inevitable. Only the saints approach the sublimity of Christ's commandment of love. The rest of us are conditioned by our own prejudices, and all of us—Catholics and Protestants—are heirs to a 400-year history of suspicion and, even, dislike. Looking at the relations of Catholics and Protestants in many parts of Europe, however, one would have to be a pessimist indeed to doubt that the situation in the United States could be improved.

I have been asked to contribute a Catholic's—a *particular* Catholic's—view of American Protestantism. In thinking about this, I see again that objectivity comes hard. We are all (I repeat) conditioned by our own prejudices. For most Catholics, Protestantism is a peculiarly inexplicable phenomenon. And though many of my co-religionists may disagree with some things I say in this article, I think they will agree with this: for most Catholics, an ordered skepticism is easier to understand than Protestantism. Obviously this is not an easy or a pleasant fact for a Catholic to admit, especially when he is writing for a primarily Protestant audience. But it is true, and it indicates something profound about Catholic-Protestant difficulties.

James Joyce expressed this classically in a famous passage toward the end of *A Portrait of the Artist as a Young Man*, where Stephen Dedalus (Joyce himself) tells his friend Cranly that he is abandoning Catholicism:

> "Then—said Cranly—you do not intend to become a Protestant?"
>
> "I said I had lost the faith—Stephen answered —but not that I had lost self-respect. What kind of liberation would that be to forsake an absurdity which is logical and coherent and to embrace one which is illogical and incoherent?"

However arrogant this passage may sound to Protestants, I think they should realize that Joyce was here expressing something more profound than Catholic prejudice or Irish insularity. He was stating a conviction almost universally held among Catholics, that there is no alternative to the Church of Rome except disbelief. For most Catholics, Protestantism, with its innumerable divisions, seems at best compromise and at worst chaos. Our own concept of the Church, with its system and logic, its tradition and order, does not prepare us for sympathy with any version of Christianity less "certain" or more ambiguous than our own. We are apt to see in Protestantism a mere shadow-Christianity, the sad example of what happens once the objectivity of Catholic authority is overthrown.

I would not argue here whether this is good or bad, but it has important consequences for Catholic-Protestant relations on almost every level. Since Catholics tend to see Protestantism as mere negation, mere *anti*-Catholicism, they tend also not to take it seriously as a genuine *Christian* concern, even in the social and political orders. From this fact much of the religious misunderstanding in our pluralist society results.

One outstanding and discouraging fact about the Catholic-Protestant situation in America is that, on the popular level at least, most of our controversies are conducted on the level of caricature. The Protestant caricature of Catholicism is a monolith called "Romanism," which is authoritarianism pure and simple. The Catholic caricature of Protestantism is that mere negation, that compromise-Christianity which it is so easy to dismiss. Because of these caricatures, Protestants approach Catholicism with unreasoning suspicion, and Catholics view Protestantism with fatuous condescension. Thus are the real issues between us evaded.

Both caricatures are obviously sins against charity and truth, and the first object of any Catholic-Protestant encounter should be to destroy them. But before this can be done, each group must admit, quite honestly, its own responsibility for creating and maintaining the caricatures. Catholics must take some of the blame for their own part in maintaining that "monolithic" caricature of the Church which they deplore. And Protestants must acknowledge their responsibility for presenting a spectacle of negativism and anti-Catholicism on the American scene.

I do not believe that Catholics generally have anything that approaches an adequate understanding of what Protestantism actually *is*. Most of them know only what it is *not*. And this is a major failure in Catholic education.

I recall my own education. It was in Catholic schools from the first grade through my master's degree, and I am most grateful for it. But I am not grateful for what it taught me—or, more accurately, for what it failed to teach me—about Protestantism.

In primary and secondary schools I learned the standard things, all negative: Protestants reject the authority of the Pope; they do not honor the Virgin

Mary; they deny the efficacy of good works; they acknowledge only two sacraments, etc. In the college that I attended I learned nothing more. (But the history department offered a two-semester course under the interesting title, "The Protestant Revolt and the Catholic Reformation.") Through eighteen years of Catholic education I heard nothing positive about Protestantism; no teacher ever suggested that, beyond the Reformation's negations, Protestantism has a prophetic vision of its own vocation. (I would note here my suspicion that, in the teaching of Roman Catholicism, Protestant schools do no better.)

If the religious situation in America is to improve, Catholics must understand—better than they have in the past—that Protestantism has its own unique genius, that it witnesses to some of the central truths of Christianity, that, at its best, it is moved by a special sense of God's awful majesty and a special jealousy for his sovereign rights. And Catholics can admit these things even though they must finally judge Protestantism to be separated from the Church's visible unity and doctrinally incomplete.

More than this, a Catholic can be thankful for the witness Protestantism bears to some aspects of Christion truth and the Christian vocation that, at various times in the Roman Church's history, may be obscured. I, for one, am grateful to Methodism for the witness it bears to the life-giving action of the Holy Spirit, and to Presbyterianism for its careful guarding of "the Crown Rights of the Redeemer"; I am grateful to Anglicanism for its deep sense of seemliness and order in worship, to Lutheranism for its emphasis on the grace of God, and to the Congregational Churches for their special awareness of the responsibility of the local community of believers in the total life of Christianity. I am grateful to Protestantism generally for its devotion to the prophetic ministry of the Church.

God does work in mysterious ways, and the Catholic should see the hand of God in all these things. One of John Henry Newman's most moving letters was that in which he declared, after many years as a Catholic, that he would "never" attack the Anglican Church. How, he asked, can any Catholic attack a community in which so much of God's truth is proclaimed and so much evidence of God's grace is to be seen?

The faces of Protestantism in America are more various, probably, than in any other country; the various gifts of Protestantism are consequently more manifest here, too. I hope it will not seem ungracious of me to say that, because of this, Protestantism's special defects are perhaps more evident here than in any other place. What the American Catholic sees when he looks at Protestantism are often, unfortunately, those things about which Protestantism can be least proud: a narrow moralism, anti-Catholicism, and what I would describe as a kind of crypto-Erastianism. (I would be the first to admit that, when he looks at Catholicism in America, the Protestant may well see evidence to confirm *his* worst suspicions of the Church of Rome: clerical paternalism and a philistine anti-intellectualism. But this is not the subject of my article.)

Theologically and historically, Protestantism and Catholicism are separated by disagreements that—except for Divine intervention—will probably never be healed. There will never be a Protestant Catholic Church, nor will there ever be a Catholic Protestant Church, at least in any sense that a Roman Catholic could admit. But of all the differences between the two traditions, few are more significant than the primacy each tradition assigns to the intellect and to the will.

The Catholic tradition stands eternally for the primacy of the intellect over the will, of the logos over the ethos; historic Protestantism has tended to be voluntaristic, to give primacy to the will. For a Catholic, goodness is for the sake of truth; for most Protestants, truth is for the sake of goodness. There seems little doubt that the intense moralism of modern Protestantism is a result of this ordering. The Protestant, almost by self-definition, is a "good" man; the Catholic, by self-definition, is a man who holds the truth.

I have no intention of discussing here the merits of either tradition, but both, obviously, have their effects in social and cultural life, and both have their temptations. If the natural temptation for the Catholic—with his assurance of "truth"—is an arrogant dogmatism, the natural temptation for the Protestant —with his concern for "virtue"—is a puritanical moralism. This is the temptation, I believe, to which a good portion of American Protestantism has succumbed, and because our culture is a predominantly Protestant culture, the American ethos has succumbed to it too.

This obviously is not something about which a Catholic has any right to complain. One cannot reasonably "blame" a culture for the way it has developed. What a Catholic does have a right to complain of, however, is the assumption among large numbers of American Protestants that their own version of morality—which a Catholic sees as a sectarian-puritan version—is in some way part of the American-way-of-life. There is a great irony in the fact that those Protestant groups that are most keen on "separation" of the church and state, and most worried about the Catholic "threat" to separation, are also the groups that would impose a Protestant ethos on the community through civil law, wherever possible. The absolute prohibition of drinking and gambling through civil legislation is, of course, the major example of this.

How is this achieved, this identification of a Protestant puritanism with Americanism itself, by men sincerely devoted to "separation" of church and state? I suspect it is by what I have called a kind of crypto-Erastianism among many American Protestants. Historically, Protestants have often embraced an Erastian theory of church-state identification. In this country they are, overwhelmingly, in favor of church-state separation. In many cases, though, they seem to be in favor of separation as a weapon against "Rome." They are for separation of the church from what they still assume to be an implicitly Protestant state.

All this is, of course, on the level of emotion. It would not, could not, be defended rationally. But I think it is operative—and significantly operative—nonetheless. On the subconscious level many Protestants still think of the United States as *their* country and fight to keep it so. But they do not see this as a violation of separation: they are fighting to keep America "American," by which they mean Protestant in its predominant mores and symbols.

I realize that I am here criticizing a phenomenon that is dying. The most responsible voices in American Protestantism have for many years been warning against the assumption that Protestantism is somehow *the* American religion and that Catholics and Jews are not quite in the club. But it takes time for popular sentiment to catch up with intellectual perception, and Catholics of my generation still feel the heavy hand of Protestant "purity" upon us in many areas of American life.

We still feel, too, the sharp cut of anti-Catholicism, even when it is "civilized," patronizing and well meant. I would not trouble the reader by pointing to the more primitive expressions of anti-Catholicism that still exist in our land and are reflected in some popular Protestant journalism—and also in some recent Gallup polls. This does not bother me or, I think, most Catholics. It is vestigial; it is almost—but not quite—dead. What does bother me a good deal is the challenge, still given us, to "prove" our Americanism, and we hear this challenge even at "advanced" interfaith gatherings. I, for one, am very tired of explaining that, no, I *really* feel no conflict between my Americanism and my Catholicism. The day is rapidly coming—I think it has come for me—when American Catholics will refuse to answer such challenges, no matter how well they are meant, and will return them for the insults they are.

What I hope for in American Protestantism is that it continue to move in the direction it is now moving —away from sectarianism, from a narrow moralism and an obsessive anti-Catholicism—toward re-emphasis on those things that are great and profound in its own tradition. I hope it will worry less about "Rome" and about such, in my view, inane issues as an ambassador to the Vatican, and more about the real danger it faces in making too cozy an alliance with the forces of American secularism. I hope Protestantism deepens its own best heritage: that its renewed concern for the Church and the Sacraments, for Christian unity and ecumenical encounter, are the signs of its future. I hope that both Catholics and Protestants will increasingly realize that we have much to learn from each other. Because, though the achievement of Christian unity must wait upon God's good time, we are all, even now, baptized in the same Christ.

• "Tour de Force of the Mind"

A Protestant Writes from Latin America to
Raise Some Questions with Mr. Clancy

Robert L. Schlager

I think Mr. Clancy is about as close to understanding Protestantism as any Catholic I have met. He describes the issues between us as a question of "intellect as opposed to the will." This very description, while true in a philosophical sense, is a very revealing description, for it is precisely the nub of the difficulty in Protestant-Roman Catholic discourse. . . .

This difficulty is almost immediately apparent in talking with priests, for when a Protestant minister tries to explain what Protestantism is, you can almost see the gears whirl as they quickly retort, "Ah ha, it is a question of Intellect and the Will!" It is just this question of "Intellect vs. Will" that makes discourse between us difficult if not impossible. . . . it seems to me that the Catholic persists in seeing religion as a question of philosophy. It is a "tour de force" of the mind whereby you prove the existence of God, the authority of the Church and the Pope as well as the rest of Catholic doctrine. And even should this impressive mental system crack under stresses of experience, it yet remains as an almost infallible inoculation against any other kind of religious experience. It likewise has its distinctive cultural manifestations.

. . . The only logical result when a man becomes disillusioned with the Church, the Pope, and church doctrine is simply disbelief. As a North American I was appalled to discover the importance of atheism . . . in all of Latin America and the Catholic world. . . .

But atheism is not the only manifestation of this disbelief, for all through society and culture you see anti-clericalism, socialism (which in these countries is largely a secular plea for justice and reaction against Catholicism), masonry, and rationalism. Voltaire and Rousseau are still taken most seriously in the intellectual circles of this world. And all of these things are but manifestations of disbelief, an assertion of the will, or revolt against the "reasonable philosophy" of the Church. And so Thomism seems to have the unique ability to create its own opposition.

What then is the problem of discourse between Catholics and Protestants? In my opinion if we are to retain any of the Thomistic frame of reference we must speak of Intellect vs. Experience of the Holy Spirit. Although this mixing of two traditions does not seem too satisfactory, it is yet as useful as anything that comes to my mind. In my own pastoral experience I have found that the only satisfactory thing is to drive back to the biblical categories where we must speak of faith vs. despair, sin, and salvation, and grace vs. works. These are the religious issues upon which true religion must take its stand. And these are the ultimate issues of life that both Protestant and Roman Catholic must face.

Perhaps as a side note we Protestants ought to notice what kind of opposition we create. The shallowness of faith and worship is usually noticed for what it is: hypocrisy, moralism, and congregational isolation. Oh, yes, we splinter off into numerous sects, but there is another side to it too. Kierkegaard was disillusioned with the Lutheran Church of his day, but his disillusionment became a despair that drove him deeper into the arms of grace. And if we call the roll of the Reformers—Luther, Calvin, Wesley, the Pilgrim Fathers, Roger Williams, and the others—the story is the same. The reaction is reform that has been a peculiar grace to Protestantism rather than the curse some think.

There is nothing short of a religious revolution that renders meaningless such terms as "Intellect vs. Will." It is simply to say that no man can truly discuss the religious issues of life until he is willing to face the truth about himself, his destiny, and God.

Mr. Clancy says the Catholic is by definition a "man who holds the truth." This we welcome, for the issue of true religion is always the *truth*. And any pastor who has not had to face this issue has never really been a pastor. But the question of truth must be taken in utter seriousness as a religious issue rather than a simple question of logic and philosophy.

I cannot refrain from making some comment upon this whole question of "moralism." This is a constant preoccupation of many Protestant theologians of my acquaintance as well as a source of irritation to many Catholics. But this is not only a Protestant problem, for those of us who live in Latin America know through experience its Catholic counterpart. Is it not really the problem of phariseeism, the attempt to achieve by law what you cannot achieve by grace? Here, of course, we do not have prohibition or anti-gambling legislation . . . but we do have such things as laws forbidding divorce, birth control information is prohibited, prohibition of coeducation in various countries, literature censorship is a constant issue, and other small irritations. Of course, these things are always said to be violations of the "natural law," but what seems so sure and logical to Catholics because of their philosophical presuppositions is to us nothing more than another brand of puritanism or moralism. And worse than that, it forces us into patterns of life that we regard as "immoral and anti-Christian."

I must confess that I am a bit baffled by the idea of Protestants espousing a "crypto-Erastian" theory of church-state relationships. Perhaps in history Protestants have espoused such a theory, but the Protestant record of fight against just this idea of state domination of religion, especially in the United States, is long, loud, and clear. Here in Latin America Erastianism is practiced almost universally. . . .

Of course, we Protestants have no illusions about equal citizenship in this area. There is no question about a Protestant being elected President. The Constitution simply forbids it. And in every court of justice we must stand before a crucifix. I mention these things not in bitterness, for I am not a citizen here and I rather expect these cultural manifestations of a long history of Roman Catholicism.

What surprises me is that Mr. Clancy is unable to see that the basic social ethics and ethos of the United States is a *Protestant* ethic and the ethos of the country is also indebted to these roots. Of course, many would say this is a "post-Christian" era and what ethics do exist in the United States are very badly practiced. This, of course, is true and undoubtedly will always be true. Sin is not wished out of existence.

Perhaps this is the ultimate revelation of a parochial blindness that many Protestants are unable to overcome, but many of us *do* look upon the United States as a country built upon the basic building stones of Protestant ethics and doctrine. If this is Erastianism, then the substance of any culture will inevitably be mixed with the laws and the men who make them. And I see no escape in any state from this sin. But with all its faults, it remains a land of freedom where a Roman Catholic *can* (by law) be elected President, and all of us have been nourished at this fount of life.

V.

ROMAN CATHOLICISM: UNWELCOME MISGIVINGS

Henry P. Van Dusen

———

In attempting a Protestant rejoinder to the admirable contributions of Father Weigel, Dr. O'Dea, and Mr. Clancy—each of them able, informed, and informative, candid yet irenic—one discovers himself in acute inner tension. Shall he yield himself to the almost irresistible impulse to rejoice in the mere achievement of conversation, to search out agreements, and to anticipate increasingly significant rapprochement? Or shall he respond to the insistence of all three Catholic participants upon the essentiality of utter frankness if the proposed dialogue is to have value and accept the uncongenial assignment to record unwelcome misgivings? Recognizing that no one, even if holding firmly to "the truth," can possibly embrace "the whole truth" within rigorous space limits, this article undertakes the second alternative.

First of all, the question must be raised of how far Catholic exponents of "liberal" interpretation of Protestant-Catholic relations speak representatively, let alone authoritatively, for their Church. If the counter-question be pressed—to what extent their opposite numbers among Protestants, e.g., the editors of *Christianity and Crisis,* speak in behalf of Protestantism—a vital difference must be noted. So far as can be discovered, "liberal" Catholics exert little if any influence upon the official and binding "line" of the Catholic hierarchy, either in America or at Rome; indeed that "line" appears pointed in a steadily more reactionary rather than liberal direction. In contrast, liberal Protestants do exert substantial if minority influence upon the convictions and policies of their churches; indeed, positions that they may prophetically espouse today often become the official "line" tomorrow.

From this a corollary follows: in thinking of Catholicism, non-Catholics cannot evade the obligation to distinguish always between the attitudes of liberal Catholics and the position of the Catholic Church. Protestants *are* justified in rejoicing over the achievement of conversation, in searching out agreement, and in anticipating further rapprochement with liberal Catholics. They are not entitled, however, to harbor the illusion that this reflects or forecasts a drawing together of the Protestant and Catholic churches. Unfortunately this is a distinction that is too often blurred, an illusion that is too often cherished in precisely those Protestant circles which on most other issues do not permit themselves the luxury of sentimental and wishful thinking.

The current vogue among both liberal Catholics and liberal Protestants is to play down the gravity if not the reality of church-state issues (where, in fact, most of our tensions are focused), to argue that American Catholics have been grossly misrepresented if not caricatured, and to join in flaying Protestants and Other Americans for Separation of Church and State as a convenient whipping boy.

In appraising Catholic policies on these issues, Protestants have often cited the position set forth by the distinguished Catholic scholar Father John A. Ryan in his authoritative writing on church and state. That position is in substance: when Catholics are a minority in any country or community, they are under obligation to conform to the prevailing law and practice with respect to religious liberty, the status and privileges of religious institutions, etc.; when Catholics are an effective majority, it is their duty to seek to bring law and practice into accord with Catholic principle, i.e., state and church in intimate alliance under the guidance of the Church's leadership.

The present tendency is to discount Father Ryan as a spokesman for American Catholics. Undoubtedly he does not speak for many liberal Catholics. But that is not the issue. Does the position set forth faithfully reflect official Catholic principle and policy? Protestants must assume that it does unless and until it is disavowed by higher authority.

While there have been reassuring statements by American bishops on the Catholic's loyalty to the Constitution, there has been, so far as I am aware, no assertion of alteration in ultimate guiding principle. Indeed, it is difficult to contemplate that there could be, since that principle is at the very heart of Catholic dogma. And, to the credit of Catholicism, what matters at the end of the day is the Church's underlying theological position.

Nor is this a matter of dogmatic principle only. The position outlined is in fact Catholic practice in virtually every country where loyal Catholics constitute a majority or effective plurality of the populace. Only one who has observed at first hand the actual situation in one or more of these "Catholic" countries can rightly appraise the normative consequences when the Catholic hierarchy is in a position to direct the influence of the Church toward bringing church-state relations into accord with Catholic principle.

Illustration need not be drawn from foreign countries only. It would be difficult to find a community in the United States where Catholics constitute a majority or effective plurality of the electorate in which non-Catholics are not continuously and deeply concerned over the character and extent of pressures exerted by the Church and its official spokesmen upon legislation and government. This concern is not confined to Protestants; it is often strongest among secularists. Indeed, it is important to stress that these issues do not pose merely a Protestant-Catholic confrontation, but rather a source of tension between Catholics and their fellow citizens.

Here, of course, is the crux of the "Catholic for President" issue. In the pre-election campaign Senator

Kennedy may have deliberately and convincedly dis-
associated himself from the traditional Catholic
conception of a Catholic officeholder. If so, he is
disowning Catholic practice in the state of his own
rearing (the Commonwealth of Massachusetts). More
than that, he is disavowing in principle basic Catholic
doctrine. In the event of the election of a Catholic to
the Presidency, "political shrewdness" might, as Dr.
O'Dea argues, restrain Catholic authorities from ex-
erting upon this high office the types of persuasions
and pressures that are all too familiar in state and
local governments. But "political shrewdness" can be
expected to exercise constraint only so long and so far
as expediency dictates.

Protestants' most serious misgivings, however, arise
from an even deeper and more disturbing fact—the
dominant trend in official Catholic thought. By general recognition, that trend has been increasingly ret-
rogressive, indeed reactionary. The latest dogma, the
"Assumption of the Virgin," is only the most recent
illustration of a lengthening sequence of official papal
or Vatican pronouncements that seem to Protestants
more and more to flout responsible historical truth,
to magnify the miraculous if not the magical, and to
steadily widen the gulf between Catholic and Protestant theologians. That many forward-looking Catholics
regret this only renders the fact more painful as well
as poignant.

When history passes definitive judgment upon the
late Pope Pius XII, with due recognition of his great

gifts, his saintly character, and his lofty devotion to peace, it is almost certain to discover one of his mightiest influences to have been an accentuation of this reactionary trend in official Catholic theology. Pope John XXIII has shown engaging originality; it is doubtful whether he could possibly reverse, even if he wished to do so, the direction that has dominated the Church's thought for most of the past century.

Mr. Clancy has suggested that the watershed between Protestantism and Catholicism is in the relative importance they attach to goodness and truth. "Protestantism has tended . . . to give primacy to the will. . . . The Catholic, by self-definition, is a man who holds the truth." No; the far more decisive dividing line is *within* the province that the Catholic claims as his own—in the conception and conviction of truth.

Mr. Clancy further gives an engaging description of how difficult it is for a Catholic to imagine how a person of intelligence and integrity could ever be a Protestant. The latter may be permitted to respond in the precise obverse. For many Protestants, the final insoluble mystery is how their highly intelligent and patently sincere Catholic friends can possibly affirm their Catholic "truth," with its ever enlarging insistence upon what, to Protestants, is incredible as well as unhistorical, typified but not exhausted by a steadily mounting Mariolatry.

Within that larger loyalty to the totality of Catholic dogma, a stumbling block with direct relevance and special aggravation for fellow Americans is Catholic doctrine on the normative relations of the civil and ecclesiastical powers. In many ways it would be easier as well as more nearly in accord with fact if Protestantism and Catholicism faced each other as two faiths, as each of them confronts Judaism.

Dialogue should further mutual understanding. It is often assumed that understanding will almost automatically advance collaboration and even unity. On the contrary, it may disclose deeper differences, broader chasms, higher obstacles. If the issues of tension between American Catholics and Protestants are explored in their full range and exposed in their wider context, especially if the foregoing interpretation of the dominant trend in official Catholic theology is correct, this may well be a first result. Nevertheless, in the interest of truer understanding dialogue is hopefully to be pursued.

• "Double Soliloquy Is Not a Dialogue"

An Outstanding Catholic Journalist Cites the Need for a Continuing and Even Wider Dialogue

MONSIGNOR FRANCIS J. LALLY

Without intending to supply it, I suppose, Dr. Van Dusen has provided the best evidence for the necessity of a continuing and even wider dialogue. Its first and most salutary purpose will be the exchange of accurate information in *both* directions. Dr. Van Dusen has his problems on this score.

At the very outset there is a distinction drawn between the "liberal" Catholic and the "official and binding 'line' of the Catholic hierarchy." This is an easy division that does not exist in fact; within the hierarchy as within the Church generally there is a variety of viewpoints on the numberless matters that lie outside of the domain of faith and morals. On what evidence, moreover, are we to suppose, as Dr. Van Dusen claims, that "liberals" among Protestants exert an influence on policy, but "liberals" among Catholics do not? The Catholic Church is both changeless and changing, and every force can claim its effect in the contemporary coloring of the Church as an institution.

Father Ryan, now more than fifteen years dead, is brought out again as a kind of "official" church-state theologian for American Catholics, something he surely never claimed for himself. On this question we are told that the Catholic principle—state and church in an "intimate alliance under the guidance of the Church's leadership"—exists in "virtually every country where loyal Catholics constitute a majority or effective plurality." It would be easier to say this of Protestantism which has many more "establishments" than the Catholic Church. How explain away places like France, Italy, Belgium, Luxembourg, Austria, Ireland, and West Germany?

Then there is Massachusetts and the perennial charge of church pressures on politics. Political leaders in Massachusetts react to the pronouncements of the Catholic hierarchy in just the same manner that political leaders in Georgia (or dozens of other places) react to the pronouncements of Protestant elders in their community. What can be said of birth control in Catholic Massachusetts can be said many times over about liquor and gambling in the heavily Protestant sections of the South and the Midwest. This is not a Catholic problem; it is everybody's problem. American Protestants have not learned something that the rest of us have long known—what it means to be a minority.

Speaking of "reactionary trends" in Catholic theology, Dr. Van Dusen cites the dogma of the Assumption of the Virgin. This, he says, flouts "responsible historical truth" and magnifies "the miraculous if not the magical." These, we should recall, so far from being new, are the same charges the nineteenth century scholars brought against the Virgin Birth, the Resurrection, and the Divinity of Christ. If "reactionary" means old, we must allow that the dogma of the Assumption is very reactionary, going back even to apostolic times.

All of this makes a single point. We plainly need dialogue, but we must be sure that those taking part in it are listening as well as speaking. A kind of double soliloquy is not a dialogue; it is not even a debate. We must learn and unlearn from each other a great many things before we will even know how the lines are drawn among us. I know this is true of editors, and Dr. Van Dusen has convinced me that it is also true of theologians.

• Simplifying the Complicated

A Parish Priest Maintains That "Complicated and Delicate Questions" Have Been "Unduly Simplified"

FATHER BERNARD DAUENHAUER

Henry P. Van Dusen's article in response to the statements by three American Catholics fills me with regret that we Catholics have expressed so poorly what we mean by official authoritative teaching and what is simply the opinion of some churchman. At the same time, I do feel that Dr. Van Dusen has unduly simplified complicated and delicate questions both of fact and principle.

Dr. Van Dusen maintains that liberal Catholics exert little, if any, influence upon the official line, as he calls it, of the Catholic hierarchy either in America or Rome. This official Catholic line he apparently equates with what is sometimes called conservative Catholicism. His observation has some validity, but for accuracy's sake he must except many bishops of Europe, particularly in France, Germany, and Northern Italy.

There is no point in denying that there is a significant difference in viewpoint, attitude, and approach between the so-called liberal Catholics and the so-called conservative Catholics. And in this country the liberal Catholics are in the minority. It must be noted, however, that this division extends to and through the hierarchy of this country, and not only the hierarchy of this country but into the very workings of the Vatican itself. Where then is the official Catholic line? I cannot go into a full-length treatise on Catholic teaching, but I do feel I must object to Dr. Van Dusen's equating Catholic teaching and the conservative approach of many churchmen.

More concretely, Dr. Van Dusen's belief that the Catholic Church is committed doctrinally to a confessional state is inaccurate. The presentation of the thesis of Father John A. Ryan as the official Catholic position is not only misleading but absolutely wrong. It is not to be presumed correct merely because it has not been repudiated by higher authority. Not all untenable philosophical and theological positions have been officially and explicitly repudiated. I would say flatly that Father Ryan's position enjoys no stronger approval than the thesis of Father John Courtney Murray.

A point, though, that I accede to in Dr. Van Dusen's article is the fact that historically the Catholic Church, whenever it has been numerically strong enough, frequently has attempted to exercise strictly political, temporal control. Dr. Van Dusen, however, errs in assigning this tendency to Catholic teaching itself. It is always a temptation of any majority to attempt to impose its will upon the minority, particularly if it can do so with some semblance of moral crusading.

This tendency is a human tendency, not one flowing from directly religious premises. Recall in this regard Kierkegaard's strictures on state-supported Lutheranism. Recall the Mohammedan persecutions in the Middle East. As Thomas Merton shows in *Cross Currents* (Summer, 1959) we all have a tendency to degrade the authentic religious message or teaching into slogans for mass movements. Dr. Van Dusen, myself, and all who are interested in proclaiming the gospel of Christ are faced with the responsibility of preventing this perversion.

• "One Unequivocal Statement of the Pope"

A Direct Word from the Pope Is Sought on the Question of Religious Liberty

C. STANLEY LOWELL

Monsignor Lally appears to resent Dr. Van Dusen's injection of the question of religious liberty into the dialogue. Rather, he seems to resent that Dr. Van Dusen does not say on this subject what he (Msgr. Lally) wants him to say.

Monsignor Lally is annoyed, as is Father Bernard Dauenhauer, that Protestants do not promptly accept the new, liberal Catholic view in regard to freedom for other churches. Come to think of it, much of the dialogue has been turning on what the Catholic Church does or does not teach on this issue. Why should there be so much confusion on the point? The Catholic Church is an authoritarian body and has a central leadership capable of making authoritative pronouncements. The statements of Father Murray, Father Ryan, Father Connell, and many others are all interesting and relevant. Yet we know that one voice outspeaks them all.

All Monsignor Lally and his colleagues must do to silence their obtuse opposition is to come up with one unequivocal statement of the Pope that he believes in freedom for all churches. I made this challenge, and Mr. Clancy cited one vague, emaciated utterance of Pius XII which, for all I could see, was no more than a reiteration of an idea we've heard before, that under certain conditions it may be justifiable not to impede error by coercive measures.

If the Pope does indeed believe in liberty for all faiths, why doesn't he just say so? That would settle the matter and we wouldn't have to have all this pull and haul over what the Church does or does not teach on this point. There is, unfortunately, no such utterance on record. Father Murray's teaching has never gained acceptance at the Vatican. In fact, the last time this issue came to a head the Vatican (isn't that the Pope?) issued a statement that pronounced Cardinal Ottaviani's reactionary views to be "unexceptionable."

Until this public record has been publicly altered, Protestants are certainly justified in injecting into the dialogue this issue which, after all, is quite important to them.

• "Gratitude . . . Disappointment . . . Despair"

A Roundup Response to Questions Raised by Protestant Writers

WILLIAM CLANCY

I have been greatly interested in the Protestant comments that have appeared in the pages following the articles of the three Catholic authors. My reactions to them have ranged from gratitude through disappointment to a kind of exasperated despair. Dr. Henry Van Dusen and Mr. Robert Schlager have raised questions that cannot be evaded in any serious discussion: hence my gratitude. They have also, I think, failed to take adequate account of some of the major intellectual and spiritual movements within modern Catholicism: hence my disappointment. But Mr. Stanley Lowell, I fear, is not the least bit interested in "dialogue"; his concern is to score debaters' points: hence my exasperation and my despair of any significant communication between Catholics and that school of their critics which Mr. Lowell so vigorously represents.

Dialogue involves men talking *together* in an effort to discover a basis for agreement; its very antithesis is men sniping at each other in an attempt to uncover each other's weaknesses. Mr. Lowell is an accomplished sniper and, as such, does the Catholic community some service merely by reminding it of the

deep distrust many Americans continue to feel for the
"Roman Church." But this service has nothing to do
with "dialogue," and I would suggest that Mr. Lowell
carry on his arguments not with those Catholics who
write for *Christianity and Crisis* or *The Commonweal*,
but with the editors of, say, *The Brooklyn Tablet*,
which represents that type of Catholic intransigence
that POAU confuses with the whole Church. Indeed,
The Brooklyn Tablet and POAU seem made for each
other because if it were not for the one, what would
the other find to talk about?

What strikes me most forcefully about the approach
of POAU to the problems (and there are problems)
of Catholicism and the liberal society is its lack of any
historical sense, its sublime disregard for complexity,
its simplistic *literalness*. For example, Mr. Lowell
seems to demand that the Pope sign some kind of
affidavit swearing that he "believes" in religious liberty. He writes: "If the Pope does indeed believe in
liberty of all faiths, why doesn't he just say so? That
would settle the matter and we wouldn't have to have
all this pull and haul over what the Church does or
does not teach on this point."

Now, really! One would think that the Church of
Rome were some sectarian movement trying to get
off the Attorney General's list. No recognition of historical complexities or doctrinal subtleties deepens
Mr. Lowell's view. It is as though a thousand years of
history had never been: all the Pope has to do is "just
say so." As for the fact that the question of religious
liberty is one of the most discussed theological prob-

lems in Catholicism today and that, as the recently published World Council of Churches study, *Roman Catholicism and Religious Liberty*, reports, for every *one* book by a Catholic that defends the "traditional" view of religious liberty, *ten* have recently been published defending religious freedom as "thesis"—these developments are ignored too.

I am thus, reluctantly, forced to return to what I wrote in reply to Mr. Lowell earlier in this volume: "Here we see the reason why most Catholics despair of any rational discussion with those who hold [Mr. Lowell's] views. . . . They will *insist* that the Catholic Church is a simple, forever frozen authoritarian phenomenon, incapable of historical adaptation or self-criticism, no matter how impressive the evidence to the contrary may be. The historic ferment and developments in modern Catholic thought are dismissed (if anything is known about them) as atypical or even hypocritical. For how could it be otherwise in a Church that is 'monolithic'? Period."

Dr. Van Dusen clearly shares some of Mr. Lowell's misgivings about "official" Catholic teaching on church-state relations and also some of Mr. Lowell's distrust of Catholic intentions in the American society. But Dr. Van Dusen's statement is (if I may use the word without sounding patronizing) serious. He is quite aware of the division within Catholicism on the issue of religious liberty; he knows that this is not a simple question of the Pope's "just saying so," but that it is, rather, a most delicate matter of historical development and doctrinal evolution. He asks, however, whether the "liberal" Catholic position is fated to be a permanent minority position, whether the "traditional" view is somehow at the core of Catholic thought.

Dr. Van Dusen's question is perfectly legitimate and I do not think any Catholic can reasonably object to his asking it. I am very interested in asking it myself. But I do not think Dr. Van Dusen's answer—that the official "line" is steadily more reactionary—is supported by the facts. Indeed, I think the very opposite is true. It is here that I believe Dr. Van Dusen fails to take sufficient account of some of the most significant developments in contemporary Catholic thought. As a "liberal" Catholic (I don't like the phrase but I guess I'm burdened with it), I find these developments encouraging.

Those of us who hold the "liberal" view of religious freedom do not think of ourselves as a beleaguered minority within Catholicism's authoritarian citadel. We are convinced, rather (and all the evidence supports us), that we are participating—however insignificantly, personally—in a major adaptation of Catholic thought to the realities—*and* the truths—of our age. I cannot think of a single major Catholic thinker of the twentieth century who does not support the "liberal" view of religious freedom, and the "official" pronouncements of the recent Popes have been clearly, however cautiously, moving in this direction. And one now hears that a re-examination of religious tolerance will be one of the major questions before the forthcoming ecumenical council. Rome moves slowly but it does move.

But important as the evaluation of "liberal" and "conservative" influence in the Church may be, I think that to examine the problem only in these terms is to fail to see Catholicism. And here, I believe, I find my disagreement with Dr. Van Dusen much more fundamental than over the question of which group is currently "ahead." Dr. Van Dusen's approach to Catholicism strikes me as hopelessly mechanistic. We might count "liberals" and "conservatives" forever and still miss the real point, which is that the Church of Rome is a living, complex organism that cannot be understood through such easy formulas as Dr. Van Dusen employs. At any given time it is probably *both* liberal and conservative, and throughout its life there runs a continuing dialectic between opposing, often contradictory, approaches to the world. Because, in its journey through time, the Church is not divorced from history or from history's contradictions. In all that is non-essential to the revelation that was once and for all delivered to the Apostles the Church argues, learns, progresses (or regresses), and adapts in every age.

Thus in our century Catholic thought has moved away from a kind of rationalism, and it is this fact that I think Mr. Schlager fails to appreciate in his valuable and generous comment. Mr. Schlager thinks that "the Catholic persists in seeing religion as a question of philosophy . . . a 'tour de force' of the mind whereby you prove the existence of God, the authority of the Church and the Pope as well as the rest of Catholic doctrine." But this, I think, represents a corruption of Catholic intellectualism that is seldom encountered in Catholic theology today, where the *mystery* of faith is everywhere emphasized. In the classical Catholic tradition philosophy is the handmaid of theology not its mistress, and those Catholic apologists who seem to reverse this order betray the Sacred Science.

Even in faith we know God as the Unknown, and to be grasped in faith *is* to be grasped in mystery. These are truths that modern Christianity—both Catholic and Protestant—emphasizes increasingly. And I am grateful to Mr. Schlager for reminding us of them again.

• "Liberal View" Not Significant

A Protestant Complaint over Being Excommunicated for Appealing to the Pope

C. STANLEY LOWELL

Mr. Clancy's stated desire to banish me from the dialogue points up one thing that is wrong with it. What is wrong is that everyone who participates is apparently required to take a loyalty oath to the Murray-Cogley-Clancy "liberal view" on religious freedom as the true and official teaching of the Roman Catholic Church. Any who persist in voicing skepticism are to be cut off from grace and consigned to

The Brooklyn Tablet, a grim fate to be sure.

Anyway, this is a new twist. It's the first time I ever heard of a Protestant's being excommunicated for appealing to the Pope.

This is not to say that we are unappreciative of what the Catholic liberals are doing. We are for them. We hope they will be able to change the centuries-old position of their church. At the same time, we must retain a certain amount of realism in these matters. Protestants must certainly not mistake the "liberal view" of Murray-Cogley-Clancy on religious freedom for the view of the Catholic Church. The fact that for every book being written on the official view of the Church, ten are being written on the "liberal view," is interesting but not particularly significant. It has not been the practice of the Catholic Church to adjust its position on such a matter to the theme that happened to predominate in the current literary scene.

It is important for Mr. Clancy and his friends to understand that some of us are really not so much interested in what he calls "historical complexities and doctrinal subtleties" as in facts and performance. If such a sentiment is irrelevant to the dialogue, we should be shown why. And certainly the position of the Popes can hardly be deemed irrelevant.

VI.

TENSIONS IN THE SPECIFIC

Up to this point, the book has dealt with Protestant-Catholic tensions primarily on the level of general principles. While those issues that evoke outbreaks of tension have been referred to, there has been little reference to specific tensions in particular locations. In this chapter we come to both the specific and the particular. The first two essays were originally addressed to a New York City dispute over the prescription of birth control devices in city-operated hospitals. The material following them is instructive for what it teaches about the problem of authority and for its discussion of the ways in which authority makes itself felt on specific questions.

• Problems of the Pluralist Society

WAYNE H. COWAN

One of the dominant social problems of our nation grows from the pluralistic nature of religion in our society. This is not a new problem, nor is it peculiar to our culture. Nevertheless, it does have its particular American peculiarities.

The problem grows essentially from the readiness of particular groups, when they achieve a majority or otherwise favorable position, to impose their private beliefs or doctrine on the total community. This willingness of a religious group to impose its moral code on the larger society is repugnant and opposes that which is best in both the Christian and American traditions.

It was repugnant when Protestants forced their view of the alcohol problem on the public domain in the form of prohibition. And we must hope that, if they continue to grow at the present rate, the Jehovah's Witnesses will not from their stronger position insist on *their* medical practices for our whole society.

New York City is currently [1958] faced with the problem that, under an unwritten regulation, doctors are forbidden to prescribe birth control devices in city-operated hospitals. Considerable pressure to abandon this regulation has been exerted for the last 12 years by the New York Academy of Medicine, an association of 3,000 physicians. It appeared that they had won a victory when they were told by Dr. Morris A. Jacobs, Hospital Commissioner for the city, that there "shall be no interference" with "proper and accepted therapeutic practices." However, when doctors in one hospital moved to provide a contraceptive device for a diabetic woman patient, who was a Protestant and whose health would be endangered by another pregnancy, Dr. Jacobs forbade the action. At this writing the battle, largely between Roman Catholics on one side and an assortment of groups on the other, continues though a bit more quietly now as a decision is expected when the Board of Hospitals meets.

To say, as the diocesan newspaper editorialized, that children who are prevented from being born are denied eternal salvation is to subordinate concrete personality to an abstractly quantitative view of human good. The question the Board must decide is not one of theology or doctrine. Mayor Robert F. Wagner seems to have recognized this when he said that as a Roman Catholic he was opposed to contraceptives, but added that this is a "medical matter" and the decision is up to Dr. Jacobs and the Board.

It seems to us that this is the only proper basis for a decision that is to be binding on all segments of the secular society. Denial of the right to contraceptive devices, particularly when they are generally recognized by the medical profession to be "an integral and essential part of preventive medicine," is a most injurious practice. Where health is concerned there should be no further question, save for the individual who feels bound personally to a tradition that holds a contradictory view.

• A Sound Decision, Doubtfully Defended

F. ERNEST JOHNSON

The controversy over therapeutic use of birth control devices in New York City's municipal hospitals came to a head when the Board of Hospitals removed the administrative ban against the practice. The decision was in line with official Protestant thinking, as well as with the trend in medical ethics and public opinion. But some of the Protestant statements issued in connection with this subject leave much to be desired.

There is nothing incongruous about the fact that in this instance an ecclesiastical judgment coincides with a scientific and professional judgment. From a religious viewpoint this means only that, in this particular instance, the medical people are judged to be morally right. But this is a far cry from the contention that *because* the doctors "approve" and "prescribe" a form of treatment, no moral objection to it should be advanced.

Since when have the Protestant churches been content to allow legislatures and professional associations to hold their proxies when moral issues were at stake? Dismayed as non-Catholics are—this writer among them—at the inflexible and arbitrary position taken by Roman Catholic authorities on this public health issue, it cannot be denied that what they had to say about the Board's decision was much more relevant in *moral* terms than the Protestant statement, with its emphasis on "proper and accepted therapeutic practices." A major function of the Church is to bring under stern review what is "proper" and "accepted" in the secular order.

Particularly unfortunate was the initial uncertainty in the official Protestant group as to whether Catholic nurses, as well as Catholic physicians, should be allowed full freedom of conscience by the hospital administration with respect to their own participation in a birth control therapy forbidden by the Catholic Church. It is to the Protestant spokesmen's credit that they came out eventually at a classical Protestant position, taking a stand for freedom of conscience all around.

But the fact that they hesitated gives some ground for the fear that Protestant strategy is too often shaped vis-à-vis the Roman Church rather than in accord with the true Protestant ethos. Whenever this happens, even the secular-minded observer will have less respect for it than for the ecclesiastical authority that is able and ready to say, as in this instance: "All Catholic personnel of our hospitals are reminded of their grave obligation in conscience to in no way cooperate with such procedure." It is more in character for a church to make judgments that most people will believe to be wrong than to make pronouncements that are sure to appear irrelevant.

What was grievously disappointing in the position taken by the Catholic leaders in this case was the complete lack of that insightful wisdom that Catholic scholars are currently manifesting with respect to the role of religion in a pluralistic culture. It is, to be sure, wholly wrong to demand or to expect that a religious body will refrain from seeking to make an impact on the entire community with its own special witness. But it is of the essence of cultural pluralism that no one group shall insist on being the conscience of the whole community. This is, indeed, a prime condition of freedom in a pluralist society; it cannot be too strongly stated that the exercise of free religion applies to groups and institutions as well as to persons and that one aspect of it is to mold the public conscience. But such freedom can exist only in the absence of organized social and political pressures to force the public conscience into a private mold. Protestants have tried this with unhappy results.

• "A Quite Misleading Analogy"

Suggesting a Difference in Kind between Protestant and Catholic Pressures

PAUL BLANSHARD

In Wayne Cowan's thoughtful description of the birth control battle in New York City's public hospitals—now happily ended with victory for the advocates of permissive contraceptive practice—an analogy is drawn between those Protestants who "forced their view of the alcohol problem on the public domain in the form of prohibition" and the Catholic opponents of birth control. Both are condemned by inference for attempting to impose their moral code on the larger society.

Isn't it time to scotch this popular and quite misleading analogy? (The bingo-birth control analogy is just as bad.) The Protestant advocacy of prohibition, regardless of its merits, was based on free discussion by free men. The policy was adopted by the free vote of an American majority after long discussion. There were no denominational compulsions about it. I know of no American church that attempted to coerce its members into a pro-prohibition vote by threat of theological penalties. I know of no American Protestant who was excommunicated for voting wet.

The Catholic policy on birth control has none of these ingredients of freedom. It has not been freely arrived at by American Catholics. Both the policy and the theological penalties accompanying the policy have been made in Rome by a celibate hierarchy that uses completely autocratic techniques for arriving at all policy decisions. No Catholic is allowed to vote against the Pope's moral judgment in the matter, e.g., by voting for permissive birth control in Massachusetts, without being branded a mortal sinner. As Father George Dunne admitted in a debate with me at the Harvard Law School in 1950, a Catholic who disagrees with the moral principles of the Pope on this question has only one choice: he may cease to be a Catholic.

The most that liberal, dissenting Catholics can do

in such a situation—besides voting a clear majority against their priests in birth control opinion polls—is to oppose enforcement of the Catholic policy on non-Catholics at the present time for reasons of expediency. That is what *The Commonweal* did in discussing the New York hospital situation, and we should be grateful for its courage, while noting that the editors saved their mortal souls by professing continued loyalty to papal principles. Cardinal Spellman's final thrust . . . to the effect that the purely permissive ruling of the New York Hospital Board signifies "a deterioration of moral life" and "perverts the nature and dignity of man," contains no hint of apology or retreat, no suggestion that the hierarchy will ever permit the decision on birth control policy to be altered by the American Catholic people.

The Cardinal, of course, is quite free in our free society to continue his advocacy of an anti-freedom policy in the name of moral freedom. But there is no reason why non-Catholics should fail to be candid about his role in our society. Our blunders are made in America by free choice; his are made in Rome by fiat. There is, in this comparison, more than a difference in degree; there is also a difference in kind. And there is, under the circumstances, no reason for Protestant humility.

• No Fear of Being Branded "a Mortal Sinner"

A Catholic Opposes the Massachusetts Anti-Birth Control Statute

WILLIAM CLANCY

In writing on the Catholic position on birth control, Mr. Blanshard states: "No Catholic is allowed to vote against the Pope's moral judgment in the matter, e.g., by voting for permissive birth control in Massachusetts, without being branded a mortal sinner."

This statement is so confused as to be meaningless. A Catholic freely accepts the authority of the Church in a carefully limited, clearly defined area of faith and morals. Consequently—and rather obviously—so long as he chooses to remain in the Church he accepts the Church's teaching on birth control. *But* this does not mean that he accepts, or need accept, the wisdom of any particular civil law in the secular society. While fully accepting the Church's teaching authority, he may still oppose a particular law as an injudicious, and in some instances unjust, extension of that authority into the realm of Caesar. So in Massachusetts, many Catholics, in good conscience, would reject the anti-birth control statute, not because they question the Church's teaching that artificial birth control is immoral, but because they think the Massachusetts law is a bad law. (On this basis, I would certainly vote against it were I a resident of Massachusetts, and I would do so with no fear of being branded "a mortal sinner." Because, as one American Catholic theologian has recently written: "Much must be tolerated by the commonwealth which in the rigor of ethics cannot be condoned.")

• "Attack against the Laws of God"

Documentation Offered to Prove That the Massachusetts Hierarchy Strongly Opposed a Favorable Vote Affirming Birth Control

PAUL BLANSHARD

Mr. Clancy concedes that Catholics are bound to accept on authority the Catholic doctrine on birth control as morally correct, and this concession in itself validates my chief criticism of "the misleading analogy" between prohibition as a voluntary reform promoted by American Protestantism and anti-birth control as an authoritarian policy imposed on American Catholics by fiat.

Mr. Clancy thinks, however, that I am confused and mistaken when I say that a Catholic could not vote "for permissive birth control in Massachusetts without being branded a mortal sinner." He contends that he, himself, could judge a Massachusetts birth control law "injudicious" at the polls with no fear of being branded.

He does not venture to name any Catholic in Massachusetts who has publicly made such a judgment without clerical condemnation, nor does he cite any statement by a single Catholic personage in the Boston Archdiocese (where the birth control referenda were held in 1942 and 1948) extending this freedom to Catholic voters. When he issues this rather pleasing— and surprising—judgment from the shelter of a non-Catholic organization in New York, The Church Peace Union, it would seem that his opinions need to be verified by some Massachusetts documentation.

The only documentation that a non-Catholic like myself can rely on in a dispute like this is the official Catholic press and the official utterances of the hierarchy. Perhaps some individual priests granted absolution to some Catholic voters who voted against their Church on birth control . . . but if so I cannot be expected to know about it. I do know that, in both campaigns, the state was plastered with Catholic posters which, in 1942 under a quotation by Bishop Thomas M. O'Leary of Springfield, declared: "Vote God's Way on the Birth Control Question—Vote No on Question 1." Also, that in this campaign the official organ of the Archdiocese of Boston, *The Pilot*, admitted many weeks before the election . . . that it had already discussed Question 1 every week for ten consecutive weeks on its editorial page, and, of course, the discussion was always hostile; that this official organ of the Archdiocese, in an editorial (October 12, 1942) headed "The Answer to Question 1 is No!," declared:

> This is no matter of simple political expediency from which by inclination or press of work a citizen might choose to hold himself aloof, but a direct and public attack against the laws of God concerning which silence or lack of interest would be a scandalous and sinful negligence. The question at issue may be resolved thus: "Shall it be made legal to assist and promote the breaking of the divine law?" The answer is, of course, irrevocably NO!

In the 1948 campaign, the opposition was just as specific in *The Pilot* and elsewhere. Archbishop Cushing and Bishops O'Leary of Springfield and Cassidy of Fall River, issued over their signatures in *The Pilot* of April 10, 1948 . . . a public condemnation of the birth control revision bill, on the ground that it would "violate basic moral principles with grave social consequences." There was no hint in any of these public statements by the hierarchy that any individual Catholic citizen could ignore his Church's directives and vote on either side for purely judicious or practical reasons.

In the face of such documentation it would seem to me that the burden of proof is on Mr. Clancy to produce some statement from the Massachusetts hierarchy supporting his alleged freedom of choice as a voter. I assure him that if he can get any statement on his side from any Massachusetts bishop, I will be more than glad to publish it in the next edition of *American Freedom and Catholic Power*. I am as anxious as Mr. Clancy to hail the unfreezing of any monolithic, doctrinal icebergs.

• "No Reason to Reject the Analogy"
Two Questions Are Raised for Mr. Blanshard by a Catholic Layman

DANIEL J. CALLAHAN

While I, as a Roman Catholic, think it very unlikely that Mr. Clancy will be able to meet the challenge Paul Blanshard laid down, at least to the point of presenting a statement by a bishop to the effect that Catholics were free in conscience to vote as they pleased concerning the Massachusetts birth control referenda, some further questions must be put to Mr. Blanshard.

The central point Mr. Blanshard has made is that the analogy between Catholic use of moral pressure and that used by Protestants is a false analogy for the simple reason that Protestant pressure is "based on free discussion by free men," while Catholic pressure is determined by authoritarian fiat imposed on the mass of Catholic believers by the hierarchy.

Two questions must be raised if Mr. Blanshard is to

be fully successful in denying the analogy. When Mr. Blanshard says, "I know of no American church that attempted to coerce its members into a prohibition vote by threat of theological penalties. I know of no American Protestant who was excommunicated for voting wet," is he prepared to offer some evidence that those Catholics who voted against the moral judgment of the hierarchy in Massachusetts were in any way under a "threat of theological penalties" or "excommunicated for voting" as they did? Granted that, from the evidence Mr. Blanshard presents, there is no reason to think that Catholics were not pressured by the hierarchy, this is still *not* the same thing as a threat of either penalty or excommunication. Unless Mr. Blanshard can prove that there was such a "threat," there is no reason why one is forced to look upon the pressure there as anything but *moral* pressure. Even granting further that, by the very nature of Catholicism, such moral pressure will have a strong influence on the average Catholic, this is still not the same thing as proving that the difference between Protestant and Catholic pressure is in *kind* rather than *degree*.

The second question has bearing on the first. It is this: What evidence can Mr. Blanshard present that Protestant pressure groups or even the official or semi-official statements of Protestant groups or councils actually represent the views of the Protestant laity? For instance, does Mr. Blanshard have any evidence that Protestant pressures against bingo in New York were the result of a vote or poll of some kind taken among Protestants? Or, even more recently, the Fifth World Order Conference in Cleveland, with delegates from thirty-three groups associated with the National Council of Churches, urged that Red China be admitted to the United Nations and that their Government be recognized by our Government. Yet Dr. Norman Vincent Peale and Dr. Daniel A. Poling objected to this statement, saying it did not represent the views of the majority of Protestants. Regardless of whether it does or not, there is no evidence to suggest that the resolution was the result of a vote among Protestant laity. And, as a resident of Massachusetts, I have not read or heard of any vote being taken in Protestant churches authorizing Protestant groups to take a stand against a proposed state lottery. Yet most have taken such a stand. One can only assume that, even within Protestant circles, decisions to exert pressure, if they are based at all "on free discussion by free men," are based on the discussions held among Protestant church *leaders*, lay or clerical, and are democratic in the same way that a decision by the Catholic Church is not just the result of somebody's whim but are decisions based on the views of the majority of Catholic bishops, priests, and theologians. In neither case is the average layman consulted. In both cases the decision to exert pressure is made by church leaders and officials. Certainly, once decisions are made, the Catholic Church has more effective means of making these decisions binding on the laity, but the point at issue here is not the problem of control but rather the *way* in which decisions are made.

If Mr. Blanshard can produce some evidence that Protestant pressure groups are the result of rank and file Protestant demands and not, as it appears, the decisions of Protestant leaders following their own consciences, then the analogy Mr. Blanshard objects to can be rejected. Until that time there is no reason to reject the analogy.

AFTERWORD

Robert McAfee Brown

———

The dominant impression conveyed by the foregoing pages is their flesh-and-blood quality. They do not discuss how dialogue should proceed. Rather, they proceed with dialogue. All the ingredients that actually comprise such dialogue are here. We find irenic essays and forceful essays. We savor the attitude of spluttering Protestants and indignant Catholics. We learn that the dialogue moves from guesses about what goes on in the inner recesses of the Vatican to guesses about what goes on in the inner recesses of the voting booth. We hear men speaking the truth in love and speaking the truth in righteous indignation. We discover that a lot of people really *care* about keeping channels of discussion open and that they are united in this concern even if they appear to be divided on almost everything else.

What "lessons" do we learn that might ease tension and further Protestant-Catholic dialogue?

1. We learn that so-called "theoretical" and "practical" issues cannot be separated. One does not really

117

understand such "practical" issues as the dispute over the giving of birth control information in public hospitals unless he also understands such "theoretical" issues as the place of papal encyclicals in the teaching *magisterium* of the Church and the way in which Thomas Aquinas incorporated Aristotelian "natural law" into Catholic theology. Those who would like to "leave theology out of the picture" will simply leave themselves out of the picture.

2. It is of prime importance that participants in the dialogue be well-informed about the faith of the other. The writers in the present collection are as representatively well-informed a group of Protestants and Catholics as exist in the United States, and yet on numerous occasions the adherents of one faith have reason to complain that they are either misunderstood or misinterpreted by the adherents of the other faith. It is one of the values of dialogue that it removes areas of misinformation, but homework done in advance by future aspirants to the dialogue will save time and energy all around.

3. It is clear that Protestants and Catholics not only disagree with one another but also have many inner disagreements as well. Protestant writers are usually just as ready for intramural skirmishes as they are for combat with an exterior foe, and the writers in this collection appear to be no exception. But it should be clear that the same thing is true among Catholics (save, of course, on matters of revealed dogma), even though they are not so likely to ventilate their differences before outsiders as Protestants are. It is of utmost

importance that the intramural debates within Catholicism and Protestantism continue at the same time the extramural dialogue between them goes on, so that the issues can be sharpened as helpfully as possible.

4. There is, finally, one wrong conclusion that might be drawn from reading the above pages. Because these pages touch on specific issues like voting, birth control, prohibition, and civil liberties, the impression may be fostered that (a) with a little further discussion a *modus vivendi* can be worked out on these matters, and that (b) as a consequence the reasons for Protestant-Catholic tension will disappear. The first part of this conclusion is true; a *modus vivendi* can be worked out, and dialogue is the way to do it. But the second part of the conclusion is false. For the issues discussed in this book are not the basic reasons for Protestant-Catholic tension. They are only manifestations of that tension.

It is good, indeed it is essential, to remove as many of these manifestations of tension as possible. But their progressive removal will serve to expose basic differences that will *not* be resolved by "a little further discussion" or even by a great deal of discussion. These are the ultimate doctrinal cleavages between the two groups, where there is no possibility of compromise or concession from either side. We need to be utterly forthright here. Protestants believe, for example, that the dogma of the infallibility of the Pope is wrong. To them it is not just a slight overemphasis or a part of a larger truth. It is wrong. They are not going to be persuaded that it is right. They believe, also, that the dogma of the Assumption of the Virgin is wrong. It compromises, if it does not destroy, the biblical and evangelical faith in the sole efficacy of Christ's redemptive work.

It is no service to the dialogue and to efforts to deal with tension to hide such facts, and Catholics for their part should be just as forthright in their estimate of certain Protestant convictions. This means that both partners must bring to the dialogue a certain complexity of attitude. To illustrate this complexity, we may refer to the attitude as one of "pessimistic hope" or (for those even less sanguine about the possibilities of dialogue) "hopeful pessimism." This description of the attitude is trying to suggest two things. On the one hand, our hope in the worth-whileness of the dialogue must not blind us to the difficulties we confront in talking together; but on the other hand, the difficulties we confront in talking together must not obliterate our hope in the worth-whileness of the dialogue. Under those conditions, there are few things more important for the facing of Protestant-Catholic tension than the continuation of the dialogue this book initiates.

BIBLIOGRAPHY:
THE ONGOING CONVERSATION

———————

The following list, prepared by Robert McAfee Brown, is intended to be suggestive rather than complete. It is limited to recent writings in English.

SOCIOLOGICAL ANALYSES. Herberg, W., *Protestant-Catholic-Jew* (Doubleday) is the best introduction to the interrelationship of the three groups in the American "triple melting-pot." Underwood, K., *Protestant and Catholic* (Beacon) is a full treatment of Protestant-Catholic tensions in a Massachusetts city. O'Dea, T., *American Catholic Dilemma* (Sheed and Ward) analyzes the issues facing American Catholics and is thus helpful to Protestants as well. Fagley, R., *The Population Explosion and Christian Responsibility* (Oxford) has the great merit of discussing a burning contemporary issue in both sociological and theological terms.

CATHOLIC APPRAISALS OF PROTESTANTISM. Tavard, G., *The Catholic Approach to Protestantism* (Harper) is one of the first and still one of the most significant attempts to discuss Protestantism from a Catholic perspective. His more recent book, *Protestantism* (Hawthorn), is a volume in the *Twentieth Century Encyclopedia of Catholicism* and is a descriptive statement of Protestantism particularly intended for Catholic readers. Bouyer, L., *The Spirit and Forms of Protestantism* (Newman) is a full treatment of the meaning of the Reformation and subsequent Protestant history, done in creative and provocative terms. Weigel, G., *A Survey of Protestant Theology in Our Day* (Newman) is a descriptive and interpretive pamphlet. The same author's *Faith and Understanding in America* (Macmillan) continues the examination in broader terms. Appraisals of the Protestant ecumenical movement are contained in Duff, E., *The Social Thoughts of the World Council of Churches* (Association Press) and Weigel, G., *A Catholic Primer on the Ecumenical Movement* (Newman). The fullest and ablest Catholic treatment of Protestant ecumenism is Leeming, B., *The Churches and the Church* (Darton, Longman and Todd).

PROTESTANT APPRAISALS OF CATHOLICISM. Pelikan, J., *The Riddle of Roman Catholicism* (Abingdon) is the fullest and most important. Without caricature it describes Catholic belief and practice and raises the important Protestant questions. Briefer but also important is Skydsgaard, K. E., *One in Christ* (Muhlenberg). In Scharper, P., ed., *American Catholics: A Protestant-Jewish View* (Sheed and Ward), six non-Catholics engage in candid appraisals of American Catholicism under the sponsorship of a Catholic publishing house. Stuber, S., *Primer on Roman Catholicism for Protestants* (Association Press) outlines the various Catholic doctrines and indicates the Protestant alternatives. Hudson, W., *Understanding Roman Catholicism* (Westminster) has lengthy quotations from recent papal pronouncements together with a Protestant evaluation. Carillo de Albornoz, A. F., *Roman Catholicism and Religious Liberty* (published by the World Council of Churches) is a fully documented and indispensable handbook to the most controversial of the "immediate" issues causing Protestant-Catholic tension.

THE CURRENT "DIALOGUE." This dialogue is proceeding on many levels. On the level of current issues raised by the problem of religion in a pluralistic society, three pamphlets have been issued by The Fund for the Republic: "Religion and the Free Society," "Religion and the Schools," and "The Churches and the Public." Single copies are available free from The Fund for the Republic, 133 E. 54th St., New York 22, N.Y. A symposium entitled "Catholics in America," recently published by *The New Republic* (1244 19th St., N.W., Washington 6, D.C.), gives examples of the dialogue proceeding on the level of political issues and religious liberty.

An imaginative and yet practical suggestion for improving Catholic-Protestant relations is contained in Cullmann, O., *A Message to Catholics and Protestants* (Eerdmans), in which the author suggests that the two groups take offerings, during the Week of Prayer for Christian Unity, for the poor of one another's parishes, thus demonstrating Christian "solidarity" even when they cannot achieve Christian "unity."

On another level, Dumont, C. J., *Approaches to Christian Unity* (Helicon) shows Catholics how their concern for unity must be rooted in the liturgy and gives examples of the ecumenical dimension in the various festivals of the Christian year. Brown, R., and Weigel, G., *An American Dialogue: A Protestant Looks at Catholicism and a Catholic Looks at Protestantism* (Doubleday) contains an appraisal of Catholicism by a Presbyterian and an appraisal of Protestantism by a Jesuit, together with an introduction by Will Herberg.

Two works of a scholarly nature deserve special mention. Baum, G., *That They May Be One* (Newman) traces in detail the papal pronouncements on church unity for the last 60 to 70 years and offers evidence of increasing openness to ecumenical discussion on the part of the Holy See. Tavard, G., *Holy Writ or Holy Church* (Harper) is a full and crucially important treatment of one of the basic issues of disagreement, the relationship of Scriptures and tradition, presented through an analysis of the medieval doctors, the Reformers, and the Council of Trent.